Emotional Intelligence

── FOR THE ──

MODERN LEADER

A GUIDE TO CULTIVATING
EFFECTIVE LEADERSHIP AND
ORGANIZATIONS

CHRISTOPHER D. CONNORS

ROCKRIDGE
PRESS

For general information on our other products and services or to obtain technical support, please contact our Customer Care Department within the United States at (866) 744-2665, or outside the United States at (510) 253-0500.

Rockridge Press publishes its books in a variety of electronic and print formats. Some content that appears in print may not be available in electronic books, and vice versa.

TRADEMARKS: Rockridge Press and the Rockridge Press logo are trademarks or registered trademarks of Callisto Media Inc. and/or its affiliates, in the United States and other countries, and may not be used without written permission. All other trademarks are the property of their respective owners. Rockridge Press is not associated with any product or vendor mentioned in this book.

Interior & Cover Designer: Carlos Esparza
Art Producer: Karen Williams
Editor: Vanessa Ta
Production Editor: Rachel Taenzler

Istock pp. vi, viii, ix, x, 130, 131, 132, 138, 139, 140; Shutterstock pp. xiii, xiv, 2, 12, 14, 40, 42, 62, 64, 85, 86, 88, 107, 108, 110, 129, 137. Author photo courtesy of © Tosha Connors.

ISBN: Print 978-1-64611-560-0 | eBook 978-1-64611-561-7

R0

*To my wife, Tosha: From leading your organization
to leading our beautiful family, I'm in awe
of your love, character, and grace. You're everything
an emotionally intelligent leader should be.*

Contents

Introduction

What is the best predictor of long-term success in the workplace? It's not the prestige of the company or companies you work for. It's not where you went to school. And contrary to what some may tell you, it's not your choice of suit pants or stylish shoes!

Emotional intelligence, or EQ, is the predictor that distinguishes outstanding performers and leaders from the average.[1] More than any other skill, EQ helps you build transformative relationships throughout your organization, whatever your role may be. A deeper understanding of yourself heightens your awareness of your own needs, as well as the needs of those you lead. Understanding how and why your emotions influence your behavior helps you make more intelligent decisions, enabling you to identify opportunities that become game-changers for your business.

This book will teach you how to apply this dynamic skill set to transform the way you lead—and the way you see yourself. Wise, practical leaders understand how to use EQ to grow their business, boost their career prospects, and create future successful leaders. If your goal is to move up in your organization, the lessons in this book will be invaluable.

I first became intrigued by emotional intelligence as a college athlete, then later while working as a management consultant for a top consulting firm. Alongside executives in the military, federal government, and business, I learned that the best organizations and leaders thrive on traits like self-awareness, empathy, adaptability, and motivation. I applied those same lessons in the leadership development and coaching work I do for executives and organizations. They helped grow my consulting career, propelling me to become an entrepreneur and a leading speaker on the topic. I witnessed EQ positively impact and change the lives of thousands of people, and I had the benefit of seeing the same reinvention in myself. It took a nudge from a highly respected colleague, a retired Air Force colonel, who told me on my final day of work with her, "Life begins outside your comfort zone. Everything you want in your life and career will come from understanding your emotions and using them to your advantage."

Your career will take flight when you start using emotional intelligence to your advantage. The best part is that it's easy to begin. This book will teach you how to implement EQ so you can revolutionize the way you lead your team, department, or organization. If you aren't there yet, this is the time to develop these skills. You'll learn the core components of emotionally intelligent leadership and apply them to your own professional development and maturation as an emotionally intelligent leader. You'll learn how to overcome obstacles and roadblocks, and how to sustain the change you've worked so hard to create.

Emotional intelligence may not be what you thought it was, so keep an open, beginner's mind as you assemble, reinvent, or solidify your leadership toolkit. Having a positive, inspired outlook, coupled with a deep understanding of yourself and others, leads to greater focus, a willingness to try, and attainment of your goals. This is emotionally intelligent leadership, and it is within your grasp.

CHAPTER ONE

Resonant Leaders

Emotionally intelligent leaders have a keen understanding of their strengths and limitations, as well as the ability to positively influence the organization and its people. Relying on research, observation, results, and interviews, in this chapter we profile four emotionally intelligent leaders in the fields of entrepreneurship, entertainment, sports, and business. Well known and highly respected in their fields, Sara Blakely, Tyler Perry, Brad Stevens, and Payal Kadakia provide outstanding examples of emotionally intelligent leadership in action, and the kinds of success that result from this style of leadership.

Sara Blakely

How do you lead a company that brings in over $400 million in sales every year while raising four young children? You work harder than everyone else. You lead with passion and love. You care deeply and understand what makes you tick. Working nights, weekends, and going all out for a very long time certainly helps. Want another answer that is a bit more surprising?

You fail. That's how you learn if you're a successful leader.

Don't just take it from me. Take it from the CEO of Spanx, Sara Blakely, whose remarkable rise to the top of the world of women's fashion is rooted in the values her parents taught her, as well as the real secret to her success: emotional intelligence.

Blakely describes the mind-set that contributes to her success: "My dad encouraged us to fail growing up. He would ask us what we failed at that week. If we didn't have something, he would be disappointed. It changed my mind-set at an early age that failure is not the outcome—failure is not trying. Don't be afraid to fail."[2] After working for Walt Disney World for several years, Blakely landed a job in sales and realized she had an entrepreneurial spirit and wanted to help others.

A few years later, in Atlanta, Georgia, she was working on the prototype for what would become known as Spanx—a pantyhose and underwear apparel company. She built Spanx from the ground up, adapting to every new challenge. Blakely used the power of persuasion to convince textile mills and hosiery manufacturers—mostly men—to produce her product. She traveled to North Carolina and used her social skills to demonstrate to mill operators why they should manufacture her product. People thought she was crazy, but she persisted, due to the tremendous vision she had for her company. She believed in herself, and her infectious passion and positive outlook drew in the influencers she needed to be successful. "I realized at that moment that it felt like nobody cared," she said. "I do not have the most money in the industry, I do not have the most experience in the industry, but I can raise my hand and [say], I care. I care the most and what can I do by caring more than anyone else does about the customer?"[3]

Blakely learned a tremendous amount about her customers by visiting stores and speaking with them. She received new ideas and valuable customer insights that informed her how to run her business successfully. She understood what motivated her customers, and how that motivation mattered for marketing and sales. It seems impossible to believe in this age of digital marketing and advertising, but for the first 16 years of its existence, Spanx didn't advertise. Blakely was on the ground and literally *in* the stores using her social skills to connect with customers and find out what mattered most to them.

Blakely has thrived, becoming a voice of empowerment for aspiring female entrepreneurs and leaders. Her success is rooted in all the times she kept digging deep to find a way to keep going after a mistake or setback. The greatest lesson from Sara Blakely's story is her powerful understanding of herself, one that was born from her experience. She's benefited from having two loving parents that she turns to for guidance, to bounce ideas off of, and to discuss her successes and failures. Most of all, her success stems from her recognition that emotionally intelligent leaders persevere, stand tall in the face of adversity, and recognize every circumstance—good and bad—as an opportunity to get better.

This perseverance helped Blakely bring focus back to the power of one-on-one communication in the digital age. Her ability to influence customers, employees, peers, and vendors, and to inject empathy into her work, has helped her gain the support she's needed to continue growing her company. She brings tremendous energy to her job every day. People want to work with her because she's so positive and upbeat, but also because there's so much to learn from her work ethic and path to success.

As visionary thinker Simon Sinek points out, Blakely empowers her team by engendering the valuable emotional intelligence principle of adaptability: "Sara's completely reinventing how business works. She brings a balanced feminine energy into business. Things like caring, empathy, and patience . . . She treats everyone like an entrepreneur. Sara tells all of her employees, 'Pretend you're an entrepreneur. And pretend you have no idea how to do this job, and you have to figure it out along the way.'"[4]

Inspiring. Empowering. Unwavering optimism and energy. A will to tackle the next challenge. Those are the hallmarks of an emotionally intelligent leader, and that's Sara Blakely.

Tyler Perry

"You're never going to make it because you're poor and you're black."[5]

Those were the words of young Tyler Perry's schoolteacher when he said that he wanted to be a millionaire and a businessman.

Good thing he didn't listen.

Perry is a cultural icon to millions of black Americans, and recently became the first African American to own a film studio. Forbes listed him several years ago as the highest-paid man in entertainment, and he's amassed a fortune of over $600 million.

But the story of Tyler Perry isn't just about wealth and acclaim. His is the story of the American dream. He has made millions of people laugh, cry, grow, and see a bit of themselves in the characters he's brought to life. His destiny has been to lift others up. The inspiration for his storytelling comes from his faith, his mother, and a commitment to being his best self through practicing self-awareness and empathy. We almost didn't get to know him, as his life was seriously impacted by a tragic childhood.

Perry's challenging and complicated upbringing defines the way he sees the world, and the art that he's given to it. He grew up with an abusive father who beat him regularly, tormented him, and inflicted extraordinary mental, physical, and emotional abuse. At 10, he was sexually molested by the mother of one of his childhood friends. Despite these traumatic events, Perry persevered by finding faith in God and an angelic friend in his mother, who encouraged him to use his faith to lift himself out of his struggles, follow his dreams, and make a better life for himself.

"I've never chased money," Perry said. "It's always been about what I can do to motivate and inspire people." Businessman, director, owner of a movie studio, writer, bestselling author, and producer, as well as philanthropist, Perry has earned everything in his career. The empire he built in the entertainment industry stands on a foundation of the values and morals he holds dear: faith, hard work, perseverance, courage, and the realization of his self-worth. He has provided opportunities to African Americans who were shunned by Hollywood. He had the courage to talk openly about the struggles of being black and trying to succeed, while also using his films to show the many challenges black women in particular face.

In a television interview, he said, "I'm the kind of person who wants to see major changes, big broad steps all at once. But sometimes it's one little step at a time that will advance you further. You have to always applaud and pat yourself on the back every time you make one step forward because it is leading you to a higher place."[6] Perry's humility and self-reflection on what's made him successful is a lesson for all of us. He's become a voice for millions of people in the black community who have identified with his funny characters and powerful themes of family, hope, empathy, and faith. He's used the art of writing, storytelling, and motion pictures to form lasting connections with people looking for someone to identify with their upbringing, challenges, and problems. He's used his platform as an entertainment mogul to share his story in an effort to motivate and inspire others to tell their own—and to realize the potential and ability they have inside of them. That's the genius of a true leader.

Perry didn't set out on the conventional business path to become a leader, but from a young age, as he once told that teacher, he knew he wanted to be a businessman. His desire to let people in the black community know they're worthy of becoming great leaders and accomplishing huge feats like he has reflects the motivation, empathy, and social power behind his words. Putting his values in action, he has made remarkable charitable contributions to the NAACP, dozens of education and medical relief organizations, and also to individuals.

Perry is famous for saying, "You're not truly successful unless your success is having a positive impact on the world." This firmness of purpose and direction guides his decision-making. Perry's belief in himself is showcased in how he never forgets where he comes from. As a leader, he famously wrote a note to his younger self to help give him the perspective to appreciate what he's accomplished. This grounding in self-awareness has led to his many successes, which in turn have provided opportunities for thousands of African Americans who may not have had them otherwise.

Climb the ladder but never forget where you came from. Always take inventory, give thanks, and be cognizant of new ways to get better. Those are the principles on which Tyler Perry has created an empire.

Brad Stevens

How did a skinny kid from Indiana with a ball and a dream become one of the most respected coaches and leaders in the sports world? By leading with a calm, reassuring presence that is sprinkled with seeds of empathy and a remarkable belief in self. The head coach of the NBA's Boston Celtics has a reputation as a passionate, emotionally intelligent leader—one whose leadership acumen has caught the attention of important scholars like Angela Duckworth. Coach Stevens, like his coaching mentor, John Wooden, learned that you can be a highly respected, values-based leader by earning the trust of your players and always having their backs, and by building camaraderie and trust through compassion, connection, and authenticity.

Every great leader needs their employees to buy into their vision, to understand their purpose and what success looks like *before* they achieve it. Coach Stevens led Butler University to two consecutive Division 1 men's basketball national title games by applying brilliant teaching technique and a positive mind-set to his program. He focused on every detail of mental and emotional preparation, as well as strategy and tactics, emphasizing how much *both* matter in winning basketball games and developing as people. Former Butler player Alex Anglin said, "His attention to detail, and making people understand why details matter, set him apart."[7]

To put his success in perspective, he was like the founder of an emerging tech startup that skyrocketed its way to compete with Apple, Microsoft, and Intel in just a few years. Butler was a "mid-major" team competing with—and beating, nearly overnight—the blue-blood, established programs of college basketball.

Stevens's gift of basketball knowledge and his ability to get a team to coalesce was undeniable. He's fond of saying, "The best leaders lead by serving others."[8] This altruistic mind-set brings out the best in the players and members of his organization.

Emotionally intelligent leaders are mindful and sensitive to how to set their employees up for success. Stevens learned this at a young age as he served as an apprentice of sorts, from his college basketball playing experience at DePauw University to serving as an assistant coach at Butler for five years before becoming head coach. Professional teams noticed when the wins and national appearances started to build. Already universally respected for his ability to keep a level head and get the most out of his players, the NBA's Boston Celtics offered 36-year-old Stevens their head coaching job. It goes without saying that it's truly remarkable to become the head coach for one of the most historic franchises in sports at such a young age.

With a passion for meeting his players where they are, Stevens turned the franchise around by building on a foundation of empathy and adaptability. With unwavering optimism, he built the nucleus of the Celtics around young players rather than veterans, molding them by leading from the heart and letting them know that he cared about them. He's an expert at tying his success—and giving the credit—to the players he coaches.

Stevens is quiet and low-key, unlike the outsized personalities of many sports coaches, but it suits him well. His players love him. His ability to discover what motivates them, what they care about, and to build camaraderie affects the player-to-player and overall team dynamics. Stevens doesn't believe in a one-size-fits-all basketball strategy; rather, he is highly adaptable at using the talent and skills of his players to the advantage of the team, and to construct a sound, strategic, and tactical game approach that leads to wins. In a conversation with Angela Duckworth, he said, "You have to be able to move on from the emotions of the game, one way or another . . . You have to be able to take what just happened as information and try to apply it and improve."[9]

Coach Stevens shows us that we can win, gain the respect of others, and do so with class by holding our employees and ourselves to the highest standard. Stevens's altruistic approach, rooted in time-tested values like commitment and hard work, helps model what the Celtics organization stands for. Serve your employees first. Serve those you lead. Lead by example, but part of that leadership should be conscious acts of serving and understanding the needs of your employees so you can set them up for success. Discussing the need to consistently and constantly evolve as a leader, Stevens presents the cornerstone EQ principle of adaptability, which is at the heart of what makes him so special: "The moment I stop evolving, I'll quit. I don't want to be a guy that stops growing. Like, I have no interest in stagnating. It's not fun. The fun part about coaching is the challenge the next day."[10]

Payal Kadakia

Don't ever tell Payal Kadakia that following your passion is bad advice. She'd be quick to point out that it's been the secret to her success. As founder of ClassPass, Kadakia melded her extraordinary business wisdom with her love for dancing and the desire to help others gain greater access to the activities they love most. ClassPass is a membership platform that allows users to search for and find fitness classes nearby. ClassPass is worth more than $600 million and has a presence in over 20 countries.

As every great business owner knows, you have to create a product that people actually want to purchase. As a consumer, Kadakia was motivated to find time in her extraordinarily busy schedule to still do things she loved. She recognized that something so intimate and personal to her also mattered greatly to others. Pursuing this passion, she found herself on the cusp of an emerging app market at a very fortunate time.

After graduating from MIT in 2005, Kadakia worked for Bain & Company, a top management consulting firm, and then for Warner Music Group. She was growing as a businesswoman, but still felt the pull back to the world of dance. She had competed in Indian culture dance competitions throughout her youth in suburban New Jersey, and this experience helped her make sense of her world as the child of

Indian immigrants. This ability to express herself freely gave her the self-awareness and motivation she needed to believe in herself, and to gain acceptance in a world that didn't readily accept her. Knowing that her real destiny lay in starting her own company, her courage was fueled by her vision and passion for something that she knew the market needed. "I think it's important for founders to be very tied to their mission," she says. "To solve problems takes time, and it's going to be a hard journey and there's ups and downs."[11] Kadakia speaks often about how much inner strength it took to walk away from a lucrative job. During a trip to San Francisco in 2010, she began to realize that her vision could in fact become a reality. But success wasn't immediate for Kadakia. In fact, what is now ClassPass first started as Classivity. Classivity struggled to get clients and needed to undergo a transformation. This led her to launch Passport, which also proved not to be profitable.

After teaming up with savvy entrepreneur Mary Biggins, the business model and vision for ClassPass crystallized and Kadakia started soaring in 2013 when she promoted a monthly membership fee, giving customers access to unlimited classes while serving as a boon for studios. Through intelligent marketing and powerful relationship building, Kadakia gained many influencers and partners.

The fear of "what if" stops so many successful business leaders and entrepreneurs in their tracks:

- *What if* this big dream doesn't work out?

- *What if* my heart and intuition have been wrong? (They usually aren't!)

- *What if* I don't have the fortitude and self-motivation to bring my best each day?

Kadakia learned from her previous stops in the business world that to get to where she wanted to be, her motivation needed to tie back to her passion for what she loves most. It was this leap of faith—this willingness to dream big and connect with her emotions—that enabled her to connect the dots between her passion, technology, and business. "I always loved business, but I also didn't feel like I was going to fit into the traditional corporate American business model. I just always had this passionate feminine energy to me, and I kind of knew that I always wanted to continue to change the landscape."[12]

Emotionally intelligent leaders recognize when to adapt, and also *how* to change. They understand that the business landscape is constantly evolving. To successfully navigate the ebbs and flows, you must have a mind-set geared toward accepting change. Emotionally intelligent leaders also have a tremendous sense of purpose that enables them to continuously work on becoming the best version of themselves. As Kadakia says, "I'd love for people to continue to live out their own personal journeys to their best potential."[13]

Kadakia's rise to becoming one of the world's most successful businesswomen was born from an emotionally intelligent mind-set that connected all the pieces in her life. By refusing to settle, and adapting to an ever-changing technology landscape, Ms. Kadakia has connected people of different races, ethnicities, and ages by giving them access to a platform for fitness activities. Her brilliant example shows us that we can serve others by also meeting our own needs.

Takeaways

The power and skill of emotional intelligence is well within our control as leaders. We can use the model of these four leaders to help guide our journeys as we build our vision and goals for achieving what we truly want most. The stories of Sara Blakely, Tyler Perry, Brad Stevens, and Payal Kadakia provide us with valuable information about the tremendous importance of persevering toward goals and through failures, leading with passion and purpose, and the significant value of a genuine desire to serve others. They're also stories of connection! All four leaders are highly adept at connecting people to the tools they need to be successful while simultaneously taking the time to listen and understand their needs. They also model the type of behavior they expect others to emulate.

CHAPTER TWO

Pillars of Emotionally Intelligent Leadership

First popularized by Dr. Peter Salovey and Dr. John Mayer in 1990, so much of how we understand EQ today comes from Dr. Daniel Goleman's bestseller *Emotional Intelligence*. The Institute for Health and Human Potential defines EQ as the ability to: "Recognize, understand and manage our own emotions; recognize, understand and influence the emotions of others . . . In practical terms, this means being aware that emotions can drive our behavior and impact people (positively and negatively), and learning how to manage those emotions—both our own and others'—especially when we are under pressure."[14]

Emotional intelligence isn't just a fad; there's research and power behind it, and the top companies in the world base leadership hiring decisions on it. We'll delve into the pillars that comprise emotional intelligence and describe how you can use them to become a highly successful, influential leader. The assessments referenced in this chapter are also presented in the back of the book; you're encouraged to use these to help you track progress toward your goals.

The first step toward becoming an emotionally intelligent leader is understanding the components: self-awareness, self-management, motivation, empathy, and social skill. From there, you can take ownership over who you are and how you lead.

Self-Awareness

Emotional intelligence begins with self-awareness, which is the art of understanding ourselves and using that knowledge to grow, learn, and improve. To understand how to influence and drive positive change, we need to first know what makes us tick: *why* we do *what* we do. At its best, self-awareness gives us a heightened sense of self-confidence, belief in self, and commitment to knowing what our potential is so we can elevate ourselves to perform at that level.

In an essay titled "How Self-Awareness Impacts Your Work," Goleman notes, "Emotional self-awareness is a leadership competency that shows up in model after model. These are the leaders attuned to their inner signals, recognizing how their feelings affect them and their job performance. They integrate their guiding values into their work. They can deduce the best course of action. They see the big picture and they're genuine."[15]

Self-awareness is also the most difficult pillar of emotional intelligence to master, because it is challenging to truly know ourselves and understand our motivations. We tend to be more comfortable pointing out ways *others* can change and improve their actions and behaviors; it is a lot harder to think, plan, and act in ways that will have a transformative impact on our own reinvention. The most significant leadership work requires that we look inward at what we need to improve in ourselves, and solicit feedback from people we trust and respect to inform us of how we lead, and how it impacts their lives.

To get the results that you want—and expect—of yourself, you need to develop a game plan powered by self-awareness, focused on five elements: your values, passion, purpose, mission, and goals. Your values are the bedrock from which you make decisions and balance priorities, and they serve as a constant in the changing world. Your passions guide your life, and leaning into them will help you operate and execute in the "red zone" so you can maximize your time spent on growing and optimizing your business.

Your purpose, or your *why*, as popularized by Simon Sinek, allows you to act intentionally, with purpose; aligning that with your mission (your definition of success) helps you clarify and do the goal-planning that leads to the desired results and outcomes that make your organization function at a high level.

The secret to self-awareness is a willingness to get to know yourself better than you've ever dared. You must be willing to go deep. Ask yourself questions such as: How much time do you spend in reflection each day? How much time do you spend in meditation? How often do you follow your intuition?

Our intuition is our spiritual guide that leads us forward—it always seems to know what's right for us. It's the voice we should listen to above the chorus of negative talk from others and the bleak forecasts that come from so many of our modern news outlets. Embedded in our subconscious memories are the experiences and thoughts we've gathered through the years. We tend to have an innate sense of what's right and wrong for us. We're able to recognize in key situations what we should and shouldn't do. The link between self-awareness and intuition is a powerful one.

Self-awareness is also instrumental in helping us combat the vices and distractions that threaten our emotional and mental well-being. Like the proverbial devil on our shoulder, temptations creep into our lives slyly, in the form of enticing offers and alluring pleasures. Only we know how we feel when thoughts and ideas pop into our heads. Should we go out late for that drink? What about investing in our professional development instead of checking up on that website that we know isn't any good for us?

Self-awareness positions us to be thoughtful and to reflect on our decisions. It's the opposite of acting impulsively to do things that won't actually help us. This is why self-awareness has become such a valued trait, because the instant gratification of "now, now, now!" surrounds us and can make us very uneasy.

Let's face it: Practicing discipline isn't sexy. Any discipline that we intend to exercise in our lives requires consistency, self-awareness, and a resolute mind-set. And yet discipline is rarely promoted in social media and our culture. It's not because of a lack of need! It's because there's nothing appealing to sell about discipline, even though it powers everyone from gamers to social media stars, solopreneurs, star athletes, and executives. Discipline grounds us and helps us understand what we need to do, when we need to do it, and how that process will help us to achieve what we want.

A lack of self-awareness in leadership can mean losing the organization—or at least losing the trust of those in our inner circle. The scary part is that when we're lacking in self-awareness, we can't even perceive or recognize the faults of our actions or inactions. Popular evaluations like the CliftonStrengths assessment[16] and the time-tested DISC tool help you recognize your strengths and determine areas for improvement. Self-aware leaders also seek feedback from peers, subordinates, and fellow leaders across industries. This self-awareness leads to mindfulness and deeper analytical thought and reflection that keep us sharp and help us stay on top of our game.

Self-awareness helps us avoid repeating our mistakes. Once we have gained the value from our mistakes, triumphs, and all our experiences, we're better equipped for anything the future will throw at us.

Assessment:
Self-Awareness

To begin, you need to understand the past and present to set your goals. These questions get to the core of who you are currently as a leader:

- What do I do best?

- What am I most passionate about?

- What thoughts come to mind when I think of the way others perceive me?

- What are the three most important things to me in my current role?

- What is my most significant achievement?

- Do I live with regret in my career? If so, why?

- Where do I see myself career-wise when I dream of the best-case scenario?

Take time to reflect; how do your answers mesh with the way you see yourself and the goals you have?

Self-Awareness Exercise: SWOT

To establish your current leadership makeup, begin with a very simple SWOT analysis (strengths, weaknesses, opportunities, and threats). List the things you do well, things you currently don't do well, areas in your life that are opportunities for improvement, and the biggest threats to your happiness, wellness, and success. Don't be too hard on yourself or dwell too much on the weaknesses; these are things you can improve upon, or delegate to others. By knowing what you do well and identifying opportunities to do more of those things, you can devote more time and energy to these areas while working to mitigate the threats to your overall wellness. That's being mindful and self-aware of what lies ahead of you.

Self-Awareness Exercise: The Terrific Trio

Ready to integrate a 15-minute turbocharge into your morning and evening routines? We're talking 30 minutes total per day, tops. I call it The Terrific Trio:

1. Meditation, 5 minutes: In silence, close your eyes, get in a comfortable posture, and clear your mind of negative, anxious, or worrisome thoughts. Think positive things. Breathe slowly and easily and focus on your breathing.
2. Affirmations and gratitude, 5 minutes: Aloud or in your mind, speak positive affirmations over your life. Give yourself some grace. Be thankful for the blessings and great things in your life.
3. Play-by-play, 5 minutes: Visualize yourself achieving the goals you set for yourself. See yourself celebrating bringing on a new customer. Picture yourself applauding a team member at the news of their promotion. See the "win."

Self-Management

Holding yourself accountable to commitments, adapting to the range of positive and negative emotions, and learning how to publicly and privately manage your emotions in a healthy way lie at the intersection of self-management and regulation. Excellent self-managers are flexible, organized, and adept at managing their time. They honor the plans they set forth for their day, knowing when to shift course and analyze changing information and emotions. This is what adaptability, another cornerstone of emotional intelligence, is all about.

As a leader, adaptability isn't optional. There's no avoiding adversity. Emotionally intelligent leaders know how to adapt to adversity in the form of employee attrition, new team dynamics, product offerings, loss of market share, and more. They face it head-on, with confidence and courage. They have certitude in their priorities, are resilient, and persevere with a positive outlook. As leaders, we're challenged to not let highs and lows steer us too much toward elation or letdown. Employees (and family members) count on us to remain cool, calm, and collected. Bringing positive energy to the equation shows the mastery of self-regulation.

I'm a big believer in "temperature checks" when it comes to regulating our emotions. Ask yourself the tough questions so you can properly assess how you're doing: "Am I on top of the needs of my business? Am I aware of my employees' needs? How can I best adapt to the business environment around me?"

Understanding how to self-regulate is one thing. Excelling at managing our time is another, and it's the key to success for the savvy leader. There's a reason that morning routines are prized and that time management apps and traditional daily planners are in abundant use; they're worthwhile investments that force us to *plan*. When we plan well, we're best suited to honor our commitments and stick to our goals. When I'm working with executive leaders, the first thing I want to know is how they manage their time. This immediately provides clarity around their plan. As we discovered in the previous section on self-awareness, this means defining the basics in your life to give you the foundational structure you need to make smart decisions, build relationships, and identify the right opportunities that will lead you and your organization to sustained excellence. Mary Callahan Erdoes, the CEO of J.P. Morgan Asset and Wealth Management (responsible for $2.8 trillion in client assets), emphasizes the importance of calendar management in making her day more efficient. You either use your time and planning to your advantage, or you get owned by the busy schedule and multiple needs from a broad spectrum of places.

Think of yourself as a "game manager" in the way that a quarterback is in football. As you plot the strategy to make your organization successful, analyze how to efficiently get things done within a finite time period. If you're leading a publicly traded company, that means meeting key performance indicators each financial quarter, along with sales goals. All leaders need the wherewithal to build in time for high-value activities like meeting with your employees and helping them develop while still being mindful of the bottom-line business results.

Great leaders also incorporate routines that allow them to meet all four human needs (emotional, mental, spiritual, and physical). Allow time for cardiovascular and muscular exercise. Find a meditation practice, or prayer, to help center you and calm your nerves so you can see more clearly. Plan the beginning and end of your day so you have a firm grasp on everything within your control. And build in time for journaling, reflection, and personal development, which can come in the form of reading a great book.

Surround yourself with positive, goal-oriented individuals who continue to push you to be better by challenging your thinking and providing accountability when needed. This means admitting you don't know all the answers—that you need a great team around you to fill in the gaps—and being okay with that vulnerability and open-mindedness.

An ambitious, highly successful Division 1 athletic director I've coached describes himself as a go-getter and someone always looking to push the envelope—a definite type-A personality. Yet the more his coaches, student-athletes, and administrators get to know him, the more they see an intimate portrait of a man who cares passionately about their success—and the success of the organization. He is a leader who is constantly self-improving, always looking for feedback to help him understand how to lead and offer reciprocal ways to help others improve. He never takes feedback too negatively because he has developed the inner strength to become more resilient and mindful of managing his emotions.

Sometimes leaders need to take a step back, even in busy moments, and allow themselves the opportunity to get things off their chest and move forward with clarity and conviction. That may mean simply taking a break. Susan Wojcicki, the CEO of YouTube, said, "I think it's really important to take time off. And I've also found that sometimes you get really good insights by taking time off, too."[17]

Self-management is more than just time management and a firm grasp on your emotions. It's "putting it all together" by being organized, emotionally mature, and programmed for daily success. As a leader, your team looks to you for guidance and direction, even when you face your own self-doubt. Great leaders navigate difficult circumstances by maintaining a positive outlook and summoning inner strength to separate desired business outcomes from personal struggles.

Assessment: Self-Management

Here are the most common emotions:

Positive: joy, gratitude, serenity, interest, hope, pride, amusement, inspiration, awe, and love

Negative: anger, annoyance, frustration, disappointment, fear, despair, guilt, discouragement, anxiety, and envy

For one week, dedicate five minutes per day to writing a list of the emotions you felt, both positive and negative. At the end of the week, reflect on your list. How did you manage yourself in the moment you experienced these emotions? Did they affect your decision-making? Your relationships?

Self-Management Exercise:
It's About Time

Do a time audit. Plan out your week as it currently is. Look at the time you spend on things that don't really matter. When you look at the things today that occupy your time, what stands out as clutter? What's wasting your time that you haven't consciously realized? Do your activities align with your game plan?

We all need to relax and decompress. I'm not suggesting you eliminate that time from your day. What I am suggesting is that you eliminate time-wasters like staying up too late texting or watching too much TV.

Self-Management Exercise:
Get SMART

Set the top monthly goals you want to accomplish for the next 12 months. Be realistic, given the demands on your time. Using the SMART criteria (specific, measurable, achievable, relevant, and time-bound), identify the goals that matter most to you. Next, fill in the necessary tasks to reach these goals.

Self-management teaches us how to use these goals to our advantage. The next time you're feeling a bit envious or stressed, pause, take two deep breaths, think with an objective mind about what you can do to better your circumstances, and go on with a renewed energy and optimism for the task at hand.

On IQ

The intelligence quotient, when combined with emotional intelligence, is the best predictor of your success in getting where you want to be and can elevate you to bolder new heights. In fact, research by Dr. Travis Bradberry shows as much: "TalentSmart tested emotional intelligence alongside 33 other important workplace skills, and found that emotional intelligence is the strongest predictor of performance, explaining a full 58 percent of success in all types of jobs."[18]

The National Council on Measurement in Education calculates IQ in this way: "Historically, a score [is] obtained by dividing a person's mental age score, obtained by administering an intelligence test, by the person's chronological age, both expressed in terms of years and months. The resulting fraction is multiplied by 100 to obtain the IQ score."[19] IQ is more aptly described as a measurement of a person's ability to reason and think. In many respects, intelligence is a gift. Through genes, naturally endowed talents, and acquired skills, our intelligence is something we can use for the greater good—or not. It's truly up to the individual how to harness this.

While it's true that more intelligent people may rise to higher levels of business due to their innate smarts, it's not a guarantee that they have all the key ingredients to stick there. This is where applying values and principles matters: hard work, discipline, confidence, and commitment go a long way to helping anyone achieve success.

The importance of IQ cannot be understated. IQ sharpens your ability to think, solve problems, and make decisions. IQ empowers your imagination and gives you your "ticket to ride" for succeeding in leadership roles. But emotional intelligence is the not-so-secret glue holding everything together as you navigate your way forward. How you adapt, your ability to perceive aspects of your environment, how you use your social skills to build relationships, and the way you self-motivate to achieve peak levels of performance all emanate from your emotional intelligence. Emotional intelligence also provides a barometer for doing for the greater good.

As we saw in the early 2000s with the downfall of energy giant Enron, a lack of empathy and self-awareness can lead to doom. Founder Kenneth Lay let greed consume him and this trickled down to other executives. Enron, in conjunction with accounting firm Arthur Andersen, incorrectly reported income and drastically misled investors. Thousands of documents were destroyed, and illicit accounting practices and corruption ruined the lives of millions. As exposed in the documentary *Enron: The Smartest Guys in the Room*, Enron's leaders were recorded at shareholder meetings encouraging employees to invest all their savings in Enron stock, right before the company went bankrupt.

Not very intelligent.

To find success as a leader, IQ and EQ need to work together. When you can combine both to increase your success, and the success of those you lead, you're firing on all cylinders.

Motivation

Picture this: You're sitting in the driver's seat for the position you've always wanted, running the show and settling in for another day of scintillating, inspiring work. Is this an alternate universe? Not really—not if you're truly motivated by the desire to live your most authentic life. Your motivation to succeed—to recognize what your intuition, experiences, talents, and skills are not just demonstrating, but making you feel—will take you far. Motivation goes far beyond extrinsic factors like money, the proverbial "corner office," or even what *you* think others might think of those benefits. It's truly about the fire that burns bright inside you, and how you link that to beneficial and worthy causes for the greater good.

Daniel Goleman defines motivation as "a passion for work that goes beyond money and status." The best leaders are exhilarated and thrilled to work each day. They want to solve problems, win business, improve their employees' experience, and serve their customers with maximum satisfaction. We're best positioned to achieve this when we're passionate and motivated by what we're doing.

What motivates you? Leaders come in all shapes and sizes. Some are extroverts, some introverts. Some lead by example, some are better at using words to motivate others. Perhaps you're more likely to have your fingerprints on everything, but another leader is comfortable delegating. Regardless of how deliberate or decisive you are, how detailed or big-picture-focused, when you understand your motivation to succeed, you'll better pace yourself for maximum productivity throughout each day. Change and tough times affect our decision-making and sometimes take us back to square one. If we turn and run away, or face challenges with a poor attitude, we never learn and improve. In basketball, they say every team "makes a run." This means that every team gets some momentum going and plays well in spurts for certain parts of a game. This is when everything coalesces and starts gelling for the unit. As a leader, think about what your "run" looks like. Where will you go for momentum and inspiration? How can you better tap what's already inside you to revitalize your spirit, link your activities to your biggest motivating factors, and ultimately achieve your goals?

Listen to your intuition. Take a retreat where you can observe the emotions you feel about these areas:

- Leading employees

- Marketing your business

- Procuring the right products

- Delegating versus doing

- Selling and meeting your strategic goals

How do these things make you feel? We all procrastinate, and sometimes with good reason. Emotional intelligence can inform us where it's best to spend our time and where we're better suited to delegate and allow others to shine. Focus your energy on that which excites, that lights the fire inside you and accentuates your strengths.

It's so important to find something that you love so much it will sustain you even when you can barely muster the strength to pull yourself out of bed and slink down on the couch to watch Netflix. We can learn a lot about staying positive and focusing on our goals from serial entrepreneur Gary Vaynerchuk. His in-your-face motivational content helps millions of leaders and entrepreneurs every week. If you find yourself in need of a spark and want to turn to a highly successful businessman, look no further than "Gary Vee."

Motivation can come from celebrating when you've accomplished something great. We should always be proud of our biggest and boldest achievements. It may seem audacious to celebrate ourselves out of concern for what others may think of us lauding our own (or shared) success. We're so focused on the grind; we're concerned about getting distracted or wasting time. We simply don't think it's important; we view it as perfunctory. We already assume we have all the motivation we need. We think it's contrived or manufactured inspiration. So many people tell me that they're unwilling to celebrate because they're so focused on the process. If that's the case, you may go a whole lifetime without taking a bow and sharing a good laugh and smile at all the wonderful things you've done!

Celebrating success gives us a booster of the necessary value of enthusiasm. It completes the cycle! Enthusiasm rejuvenates our souls, giving us the passion and power to keep moving forward for the next challenge.

While blindly following our passion is a fool's errand, following what we love with a game plan and a hard work ethic yields great results. Every great venture begins with, and is sustained and powered by, enthusiasm. Having a *passion* for what we do is essential if we want to do great things.

What if you viewed each day as your next great moment? Instead of just showing up and going through the motions, decide to give maximum effort with a positive attitude. That gives you 365 days per year to be renewed with optimism and motivation for your next great move. We always control our attitude and effort. That alone is a very empowering thought! Motivation is within our control, whether we gain energy from being around inspiring people or generating it on our own. We have to rally ourselves out of bed each day, get into our morning routine, and come in truly excited to dive into the process while keeping the big picture of our dreams on display.

Assessment:
Motivation Pulse Check

Honestly answer the following five statements on a scale of 1 (not at all) to 5 (completely):

- I am energized by helping employees develop personally and professionally.

- I take an interest in coaching others, enabling them to solve problems and achieve solutions through their own self-discovery.

- I keep a positive outlook regardless of present challenges or difficult circumstances.

- I am driven and summon the energy every day to compete to be the best I can for myself and those I lead.

- I take delight in the accomplishments we reach together as a team.

Spend some time analyzing each of these answers and identify specific examples of when you've felt this way. What do you like? What would you improve?

Motivation Exercise: Vision Board

Imagine the vision of yourself that you dream about. Who are you and what do you look like standing in the winner's circle of your life and career? List 5 to 10 attributes of that future person.

Next, find 3 to 5 images that light the fire inside of you and inspire you to be the person you want to be. Have them align with that ideal future person. Refer back to the images at least once per day. Use them to inspire and motivate you on the good and bad days. Motivated and inspired leadership, with a vision of your goals, is the best kind.

Motivation Exercise: For the Benefit of Others

Now let's turn to those you lead. List no more than 20 direct reports and top people that roll up to you in your organization.

Next, list your top motivating factors for each person. This will help you frame the *why* and *what* behind your motivational desire to help your team succeed. Focus on two motivating factors:

1. Helping them be successful for the organization and produce shared goals.
2. Helping them be successful for themselves to attain their personal/professional goals.

If you don't know the answers, set up 30-minute meetings to ask these questions. Send the questions in advance, if that could help. Invest in their personal and professional development with energy, passion, and genuine concern.

Empathy

President Theodore Roosevelt famously said, "People don't care how much you know, until they know how much you care." Let that one simmer. Within the wisdom of those words is the power that lies in empathy.

Empathy is "the capacity to understand or feel what another person is experiencing from within their frame of reference, i.e., the capacity to place oneself in another's position."[20] Empathy isn't possible if we're unwilling to focus, listen, and connect on an emotional level. Empathy is pure, sincere, authentic, and inviting. As journalist and author Daniel H. Pink says, "Empathy is about standing in someone else's shoes, feeling with his or her heart, seeing with his or her eyes. Not only is empathy hard to outsource and automate, but it makes the world a better place."[21] The best part is that empathy is a skill we all can cultivate.

Empathy builds relationships, creates new opportunities to collaborate with people you want to work with, and helps you lead with greater love and passion. Empathy, understanding, and positive encouragement are the best operating bases from which to teach people. When you genuinely care for others, they know it. Few leaders exemplified this better than the late Herb Kelleher, founder and CEO of Southwest Airlines, who once said, "The business of business is people."

When you begin each day, as you think about your goals, dreams, and ambitions, take the time to give thanks for the colleagues you have. Think about one way you can help someone and be willing to listen. Admiration and respect for the people we lead matter tremendously. Think about how you feel when someone applauds or congratulates you after you deliver a presentation. Deep down, we yearn for validation. It feels good. You'll find that you inspire others *and* yourself when you are a person of empathy and integrity. To form deep connections, show from the beginning that you care about those you lead—beyond a shared objective. Southwest Airlines was founded on the premise that they could "democratize the skies" and enable many more people to fly for the first time. Sure, their low prices and "point to service" model helped, but it was the culture Kelleher engendered and wove into the fabric of their values, mission, purpose, and vision that contributed powerfully to their success. There's a reason Southwest's New York Stock Exchange ticker symbol is "LUV." From the top down, their fearless leader led from the heart—with love, compassion, and empathy. He let everyone at the airline know that he cared, and he took the time to listen and build relationships that mattered.

Daniel Goleman identifies three types of empathy:

- Cognitive, which is about perspective-taking, meaning that we take the time to understand how someone else feels

- Compassionate, which stirs emotion inside of us and promotes a desire to want to help others

- Emotional, which is when you actually take on and absorb the emotions of someone else and experience them for yourself

All three types of empathy encourage us, first through listening, to show concern. They're so important for leadership. It's far less about "solutioning" and problem-solving the moment. There's a time and place for that. Your employees are looking for a leader who first understands, and then helps, according to that knowledge.

We develop more empathic responses the more we get out and make contact. Let's face it: Leadership is a contact sport. You have to interact with the people you lead. Empathy implores us to have a helping mindset that is by nature outward-seeking, in an effort to help others. No matter how introverted or extroverted you are, if you live with a servant leader's heart, you will make a difference in the lives of others.

Servant leadership is defined as "a philosophy and set of practices that enriches the lives of individuals, builds better organizations, and ultimately creates a more just and caring world."[22] This concept was first written about by Robert K. Greenleaf in 1970, yet its popularity has increased significantly in organizations in the past 15 years.

Successful leaders are respected and admired by others because they give without the expectation of anything in return, like former professional football player Warrick Dunn, now a part owner of the Atlanta Falcons. Dunn's acts of service for others have given families a remarkable opportunity for a second chance at living the American dream. He takes the time to put himself in others' shoes and leads with love and service. Dunn empathizes with single mothers because he is the child of one, who was unfortunately killed when he was a young boy. He became the head of household for his family when he turned 18, raised his siblings, and learned the leadership traits that he espouses today in the remarkable charity work he does.

We can all lead with genuine care and love for others and show empathy in the face of remarkable adversity like Warrick Dunn. It takes stepping out and putting ourselves in a position to help others when they need it most.

Assessment: Empathy

Identify 5 to 10 people in your organization whom you know, respect, and count on to give you objective feedback. Ask them to answer the following five questions on a scale of 1 to 10, with 1 being the lowest or least and 10 being the highest or most.

- How well do I listen?

- Do I take the time to understand others' positions?

- Do you feel I have invested in others' personal and professional development?

- Do I listen without trying to fix the problem?

- Am I sensitive, compassionate, and caring toward the people I lead?

Empathy Exercise: Coach's Corner

As an executive coach, I help executives add a coaching tool to their leadership approach. Follow these three tips to adopt a coaching mindset in meetings:

- Start a list of "what?" questions that zero in on ways for your business to become more "people-centric." (e.g., "What obstacles are standing in our way of implementing our new wellness program?", or "What outcome would be the best-case scenario?")

- When you ask each question to members of your organization, focus on active listening. Make notes. Don't skip ahead to the next question. Immerse yourself in the moment.

- Help those you lead figure out solutions related to these questions. Don't jump in and problem-solve. Help them arrive there through their own self-discovery. Keep asking more specific questions.

Empathy Exercise: Shadow

Get out there in the field! Do a job shadow of employees in specific roles in your organization that you want to learn more about. Spend half a day shadowing the employees as they work. Ask insightful questions, inquire what they need to perform their jobs better, and see if there are ways you can connect teams cross-functionally to better solve problems and help one another.

First and foremost, listen. Show you care. Be the conduit that connects people across divisions and departments by adding a personal, human touch to the day-to-day work schedule.

Social Skill

Your ability to influence the people around you leads to the best relationships and opportunities of your life. Social skill is the composite of several core components of emotional intelligence. When self-awareness, empathy, motivation, and self-management coalesce, we have the confidence and assuredness to influence and engage others in an impactful way. The question then is whether we use this cultivated power in an altruistic manner or strictly for our own vanity or self-interest. Emotionally intelligent leaders have a servant's heart and are able to satisfy their own needs and wants while also serving the needs and wants of those they lead.

Our ability to form deep, lasting connections with people separates us as leaders. Sara Blakely's ability to resonate with her staff, to act as a servant leader, and truly connect in an authentic way helped her build Spanx into a multi-billion-dollar enterprise. When it comes to product and business success, it's almost a given that quality matters immensely. No stone unturned, no detail missed, right?

But what about the people side? To get people on board with our vision and mission as Sara did, we need to connect on a level that is transformative and not transactional. We must take the time to get to know our people, show them that we care, and that our success is their success. This is true desire and hustle, born from a positive attitude and mind-set that is rooted in empathy and a desire to help others.

Former surgeon general of the United States, Dr. Vivek Murthy, a man who dedicated his life to the medical care of thousands of patients, realized while serving his country that emotional wellness should be at the forefront of our nation's health needs. While serving under President Obama, Dr. Murthy's transcendent work and research in emotional intelligence helped move the United States forward by sparking conversation around mental and emotional health matters.

Traveling across the country, he engaged in dialogue with citizens to understand what really mattered to them. He wanted the unfiltered truth to understand ways to combat illness and improve our understanding and aptitude around emotional triggers and why they matter. Murthy discovered that the public wanted more resources and assistance around mental health, ways to combat anxiety, stress, and depression, and a general awakening to the power of emotional intelligence pillars like self-awareness and self-regulation. In these discussions, Murthy learned that if we're to truly master our emotions, we have to be educated. We have to be aware of how to accentuate the positive and manage the negative so it doesn't destroy us. Through reaching out and communicating with Americans across the country, he used his social skill to make emotional intelligence the centerpiece of his platform for greater good.

Very few leaders succeed without consistently showing their employees that they care. The best work environments and companies are ones where the strength lies in the philosophy of everyone working to make everyone else around them better. I often write about leading from the heart. To me, this is the essence of mastering social skill and becoming an emotionally intelligent person. We have the choice to make decisions with our head and heart in life. The most balanced, successful leaders understand the bottom line while also recognizing that the bottom line puts their people first. To get the most out of their employees, leaders need to give the most back to them, to recognize and reward behavior that aligns with company values and principles, to invest time in getting to know people throughout the organization, and to always treat them with dignity, respect, and kindness.

The Golden Rule has stood the test of time largely because it puts us on a level playing field of reaching and touching each individual. Whether we're a winning basketball coach, the nation's leading doctor, or the CEO of a clothing company, part of our "business plan" should be assigning a high value to the people we lead. When they can see that your words align with your actions, they will help you carry out the mission of the organization.

Dee Poku-Spalding is an example of a charismatic leader who built a thriving membership platform for female leaders. She is the CEO and co-founder of WIE (Women Inspiration and Enterprise), and has connected female leaders with the tools they need to become more successful. In her words: "I'm very efficient when it comes to socializing. I have criteria I use to decide what I'm going to do . . . The first is, *Am I going to meet people there who will be helpful for what I'm trying to do?* The second is, *Am I seeing people who are really meaningful for me?*" She continues, "I used to take no and rejection very seriously and personally, so the first mantra is: 'No just means there's a better yes coming.' It really is true. Something better always comes along in a different form. My other is, of course, 'the key to your success is the power of your network.'"[23]

CEO Herb Kelleher's social wizardry built Southwest Airlines into a paragon of what it means to put people first. Everything Kelleher did looked unconventional, but in reality it was his values-based leadership approach, with consistently applied principles, that showed his employees that their needs and wants came first at Southwest. Kelleher's social genius was in recognizing the importance of employee engagement and culture, and that culture's integral importance in helping transform the business. By putting his people first, Kelleher gained the support of motivated, empathetic, passionate employees who came to revere him, and did everything they could to make the customer experience first class. How else do you explain Southwest Airlines achieving 47 consecutive years (as of this writing) of profitability in one of the most competitive industries in all of business? Yes, that's correct: Southwest Airlines has turned a profit every single year that it's operated as a company.

Emotionally intelligent leaders recognize that it's not all about profit and loss. It's not only the bottom-line numbers that matter. Perhaps more than any leader who's ever graced the American business landscape, Kelleher recognized that it's employees first and customers a very close second. This may seem counterintuitive at first, but it's this empathetic and altruistic mind-set that enables the customer experience to happen. You see, it's truly reciprocal.

In order to have "raving fans," as the business expression goes, we first need to inspire, create energy, and stir the positive emotions of the people we lead. This social skill should be a focal point for every emotionally intelligent leader. Without it, we'll find ourselves standing on the outside of the very people we aim to lead. With it, we'll have the support of every person we need to help us achieve our vision. And by doing so, they'll turn our customers into enthusiastic supporters of our business.

Assessment:
Social Skill

The statements below are probably true to some degree, but how can you improve? Think honestly about how well you are doing these things, and identify ways to improve:

- I am skilled at persuading colleagues on an idea I believe will help our organization.
- I make influencing the people I lead a focal point for gaining support in the organization.
- I devote time each day to cultivating existing relationships in my inner circle.
- I see myself as a servant leader.
- My colleagues say that I take the time to get to know and understand their needs.

What do you like about the current state of your social skills? What would you improve?

Social Skill Exercise:
Personal Greeting

Identify 10 people you plan to prioritize outreach to this upcoming week. They could be people in your inner circle, former or current colleagues, friends, or family members. Craft a personal, handwritten note to these 10 people and let them know that you've been thinking about them and would love to catch up soon, either virtually or in person. Give them your full presence and attention. Let them know you care and that you'd like to help them any way you can, either personally or professionally. Let your authentic voice shine, showing your altruistic, servant leadership that lets others know that you are leading from the heart. Then watch the positive vibes flow into their life—and yours.

Social Skill Exercise: Pleased to Meet You—I Have an Idea!

Set up a monthly lunchtime "social hour" for your division or department. Provide lunch if possible, and split people into teams to focus on getting to know one another.

- Start with funny icebreakers beyond the conventional and go for things like, "What's the worst movie you've ever seen?" Humor should get the party started.

- The goal is to get people sharing free-flowing ideas on a range of topics that can improve organizational culture, efficiency, meetings, strategy, project management, innovation, marketing, sales tactics, etc.

Keep it fun and easy. Try having someone new direct the event each week and lead discussion. Empower everyone to speak up.

Takeaways

Emotional intelligence is a skill set you can use to your advantage right away. Listen and show others that you care. Find ways to motivate yourself and learn more about who you really are. Spend time in reflection and deep thought on how emotions impact your leadership. Dedicate the time to forge connections with those you lead.

You now know what comprises your EQ game plan and why this matters in building self-awareness. Start by looking within. Develop the maturity and discipline to strengthen your self-management. Your best motivation comes from within and is charged with passion and a positive outlook that believes in the accomplishment of your goals.

With the pillars of emotionally intelligent leadership in place, we're ready to learn about the styles of EQ leadership, and to put them into practice in our careers.

CHAPTER THREE

Leadership Styles

What does leadership mean to you? The word is thrown around so often by people in all walks of life, it feels like it has a nebulous meaning. We probably all have an image in our mind of what a leader is, whether it's a cultural icon or a leader we have personally known. It's likely someone who has touched our lives with kindness, selflessness, and authority. As defined by Merriam-Webster, the transitive verb *lead* means "to guide on a way especially by going in advance."

If we as leaders guide the way and go before others, we need to determine our leadership style. In this chapter, we delve into the six distinct emotional leadership styles as defined by Daniel Goleman, Richard Boyatzis, and Annie McKee in their seminal 2002 book, *Primal Leadership*. An assessment at the end of this chapter will aid you in discovering your own unique leadership style. Maybe you'll see some of yourself in one of the six styles discussed here. The goal is to "know thyself" in an intimate, emotionally intelligent manner so you can positively influence and impact your organization.

Visionary

A visionary leader sees potential where others do not. Visionary leadership is for dreamers and doers alike, and it's inspired by the creative imagination. As Walt Disney famously once said, "If you can dream it, you can do it." This mantra propels visionary leaders forward and serves as the fuel that powers their engine. Visionary leaders set a grand course before them and use their powerful self-confidence and eye for change to bring others along with them on a magnificent journey. Every great organization should have a guiding vision, and it is the visionary leader's mission to see that the vision is attained.

Visionary leaders do three things particularly well:

They listen. Through empathy and a desire to understand what will motivate people to join them on the journey, visionary leaders practice deep listening. They let their followers know how important they are, and how valued their input is. They solicit feedback on what's working and what's not. Every day they ask, "What can we do to get better?"

They care passionately about their culture, which is another way of saying they care about the welfare of their people. They're able to clearly articulate where they want to go, as well as the significance of *why* this will benefit their employees and the organization as a whole. They're in the business of people as well as strategy and unique ideas, because they know that is business at its finest.

They anticipate change and are well prepared. In other words, they have a plan. They're crystal clear on their strategy and the fundamentals that lead to a successful business operation: vision, purpose, mission, and values. They set the bar high for goals and can adapt their strategy to the ever-changing market. They're nimble and flexible. The world is littered with great ideas that soared like a rocket at first but then plummeted to the ground and weren't picked up and converted into something greater. Visionary leaders back their vision with grit and drive.

What is drive? It's the foundational result when ambition meets enthusiasm meets belief. Without a leader's drive to succeed, even the best product or idea will fall flat. A visionary leader's ambition must continuously power their enthusiasm, which renews employees' belief that they're doing something special. This journey is as much emotional as it is mental, and it's a challenge for a visionary leader to bring their best in these areas every day.

Pierre Omidyar, the founder of eBay, was born with the gift of inspirational leadership guided by clarity. Using his vision and ability to lift others up with him, Omidyar created an online marketplace for millions of people to buy and sell, well, everything. eBay is as synonymous with the modern-day internet marketplace as Starbucks is with coffee stores. Omidyar's visionary thinking turned eBay into one of the most formidable tech giants on the planet. Describing his leadership style, he says, "Instead of telling my executives what to do, I should try to inspire them with a vision of where we're going and let them translate that in their own terms, based on their own experience, their own expertise. Inspiration is much more effective than delegation."[24]

He had a vision for success; in his own words, he desired to "expand opportunity to as many people as possible so they can reach their potential."[25] Omidyar clearly articulated his message to the people he needed to help him. He had a keen self-awareness around how his vision would be successful. He understood what he wanted to see in the marketplace, and grasped the art of how to convey that to the team he relied on so heavily. He was always willing to give up the reins to people he trusted. He let former CEO Meg Whitman do her job without micromanaging every part of his business. Under her tenure, eBay flourished and grew exponentially, becoming a multi-billion-dollar company.

Persuasion, in its purest and noblest form, is part of passion, which is a huge element of emotional intelligence. Successful visionary leaders stoke the fires inside people they lead to get them on board with their vision. They also understand and perceive what motivates them—what they value. According to an article in *Harvard Business Review*, "...people will only take ownership of strategic change if they are consistently persuaded by its value."[26] When those qualities tie back to business objectives, you have a winning combination. The article continues: "Visionary leadership is not just important for senior managers; it also matters for middle and lower level managers who play a key role in carrying out strategic change. Their ability to inspire their own teams and create strategic alignment—a shared understanding of and commitment to the company's strategy—within them is a core element in successful strategy execution."[27]

Lynda Weinman is an inspirational launching point for leaders aiming to bring their skills, experiences, and passions to the masses. Weinman began at the grassroots level; she was a graphic arts professor who loved teaching. While she was teaching, she recognized the potential of her expanding field and decided to get hands-on and build the future. She began writing columns in a monthly magazine series about web design. Those columns became the foundation of an industry-changing book, *Designing Web Graphics*, which sold hundreds of thousands of copies. From there, she knew she was on to something. She created Lynda.com in an effort to share her passion and enthusiasm for web design with the world.

That passion developed into a billion-dollar company aimed at improving people's lives in the Internet age. Lynda Weinman started by focusing on ways she could help people, which spawned a brilliant idea that enabled her to set goals and see them through to fruition. She brought others along by demonstrating her knowledge, passion, positive attitude, and belief in her idea.

Her remarkable vision was born from seeing something that the marketplace couldn't yet see. In the same way that Apple created products we didn't even know we wanted, Weinman saw the future of online learning evolving before her eyes. Her vision of a new way to learn paved the way for countless entrepreneurs and leaders.

Coaching

Lead with a servant's heart for your employees and customers and you will reap the profits you've dreamed about. The "How can I help you?" attitude becomes a way of life for the coaching leader, because this mind-set attracts the right relationships, which lead to the right opportunities. The right opportunities, when executed with intelligent strategy, yield sustained growth. Beyond the business benefits, coaching leaders empower their employees and ask them to think deeper about their development and future than they have before. The coaching leader knows that the organization's goals can be achieved when there is symmetry with the individuals' goals. This relationship is best when it works in a reciprocal manner.

Coaching leaders help employees see the greatness inside themselves. They provide unique perspective and insight by partnering with their employees to determine how they can get from where they are to where they want to be. Coaching leaders are highly skilled at breaking down the steps from point A to point B into clearly defined tasks that become milestones that match up with an individual's personal development plan.

Coaching leaders are servant leaders. Empathy, altruism, and vulnerability are baked into this leadership style, and these leaders approach each situation with this mind-set and with the goal of touching the hearts of the people they lead and learning what's going on in their personal lives. To achieve this, they build in time for weekly meetings or connections with people and know they're investing those minutes to truly get to know someone. These leaders know that investing in the people they lead is among the best ways they can spend their time as a leader. It perfectly complements their strategic, productive side with a human element that seeks connection.

The best opportunities arise when people recognize a genuine desire to help others without the expectation of anything in return. This attitude naturally attracts the right people. Coaching leaders know that the more they exercise this muscle, the less they worry about personal returns, which actually takes the pressure off their ability to lead.

In sports, just like in life, there are always new nuggets of wisdom, bold technological breakthroughs, and advances in thought leadership.

However, one constant remains: We always have control over two things: our attitude and our effort. Few leaders understand and embody this maxim better than two-time national-championship-winning coach Jay Wright. Coach Wright has mastered the ability to communicate this to his players, motivate and discipline them, and execute this maxim. His team, the Villanova University Wildcats, is the most successful and dominant college basketball team of the past five years. He starts with attitude and a foundation of values: Everyone cares for and inspires one another to be their best. He says, "In any organization, a leader's job is to make sure everyone feels confident in their role and that the role is valued. This gives everyone their best chance to compete at the highest level."

So much of Wright's approach to the game is emotional and mental. He gives his players creative freedom while simultaneously instilling rigorous discipline around fundamentals. He implores them to care for one another, to play selfless basketball, and to lead with a positive attitude. Two national championship titles in three years tell the full story: his philosophy around positive attitude, discipline, and empathy works. Sure, he knows the Xs and Os extremely well, but that knowledge is implied for leaders. IQ will get you a seat at the table, no doubt. But whether we're talking about Division 1 college basketball or leading the sales organization for a large technology company, it is emotional intelligence that will help you advance further. Wright notes, "I learned how important the right attitude is. It's a concept that permeates everything you do . . . We all bring our attitude to every situation. How do we walk into a room? How do we meet people? How do we respond to challenges? To adversity?"[28]

At the biggest stages of competition, it's not always about strategy. It's about how much we want to succeed. How powerful and indomitable our spirit is. How *willing* we are to do what it takes to win. Think about this in terms of being a coaching leader. You can have the best strategy in the world, but it won't matter if your employees don't buy in. Coaching leaders appeal to people's positive emotions in an authentic, genuine way by taking the time to get to know them and understand what motivates them. Coaching leaders consider their employees' goals *their* goals. They create a dynamic relationship of shared success that permeates the organization.

A broader point here about coaching leaders—and every great leader for that matter—is the time they spend **investing** in their employees.

Coaching leaders inspire others to create their own personal and professional vision, mission, and goals. Their authentic leadership helps light the fire in those they lead by dedicating time to their personal and professional development. They provide examples of their successes and failures, and explain how they came out better for each one. A coaching leader's greatest gesture is to give employees the gift of self-discovery, to help them think bolder and more ambitiously than they ever have before. They empower people with new information, new ideas, and partner with them on strategy, but they allow their people to discover what it means to be a true leader for themselves. That's the mark of a great coaching leader, and one of the most powerful examples of the human spirit of connection.

Affiliative

The affiliative leadership style begins with harmony. As we found in the story of Herb Kelleher, Southwest Airlines succeeded by putting its people first. It was common for Kelleher to show up at airports at 4 a.m. with doughnuts for mechanics. He'd visit Southwest gates and speak with company employees to get to know them better. At the heart of his people-first mind-set was relationship-building. He wanted to personally connect with every one of his employees and let them know he cared. In good times and bad, he was the public face and led with his famous "warrior spirit," one of the core values of the airline.

An affiliative leader builds relationship capital and manages conflict as it arises within a team. Think about your workplace; you may be in a matrixed, non-hierarchical environment where you need to rely on people you wouldn't normally interact with. So many workplaces today are *siloed*, and workplace culture can suffer. An affiliative leader bridges communications gaps, enables managers and employees through empathy and empowerment, and steps in to mediate when necessary. Affiliative leaders take the time to understand the job functions of everyone they lead so they can best determine paths forward and outcomes that are mutually beneficial for all—and to the advantage of the organization's goals.

Affiliative leaders place a high value on the emotional wants and needs of the people they serve. Just as they are clear on their own emotional needs and wants, they give that gift to those they serve. They preach positivity and are experts at communicating with each individual, showing empathy, and building relationships. The flip side of these positive aspects of leadership can appear when complex challenges and issues come up, such as the need to address an underperforming employee who is a great team member, or a high performer who is causing consternation and dissension on the team. It can be difficult for affiliative leaders to remove their emotional investment from situations that require them to judge impartially. They're such caring, encouraging, and upbeat people by nature that it can be hard to be the "bad guy," even when it's necessary.

We cannot do it all for someone else. We can't do their job and ours. Each person in a business or personal relationship has to do their best to meet in the middle and give of themselves to make things work. Affiliative leaders understand this, and do their best to create synergy between those they lead. They give the people they work with the power of knowing what they know. As they give away their talents to others, they reap positive returns that have a ripple effect. Teaching, listening, and empowering others creates a bond that leaves a positive imprint. It helps reduce stress, eases organizational tension, and lets people know that you are a well-intentioned leader who cares.

It's the selfless act of listening, leading with empathy, and creating harmony that produces a compound effect in our own lives. When we teach and instruct others, we retain that information for ourselves through repetition and rote memory. When we act kindly and graciously to improve someone's life, we find that others often do the same for us. Affiliative leaders are cognizant of what they can give and build stronger, healthier teams. Concerned with maximizing their own output and maintaining a positive mind-set for others, they don't have time to sweat the small stuff.

Take this, as observed by the Greater Good Science Center at University of California, Berkeley: "A recent article published in *The Journal of Positive Psychology* by Daryl Van Tongeren and his colleagues sought to examine this relationship [how kindness and happiness help us find purpose]. In a preliminary study, the researchers asked over 400 participants to report on how frequently they engage in different altruistic behaviors (such as volunteering) and how meaningful their life feels. Participants who were more altruistic reported a greater sense of purpose and meaning in their lives."[29]

Satya Nadella followed Steve Ballmer as the CEO of Microsoft. To say that he had big shoes to fill would be putting it mildly. Leading one of the world's largest companies, founded by Bill Gates, one of the most iconic, celebrated leaders of all time, means that you feel the presence of your predecessors. In so many ways, Nadella is the perfect leader for these turbulent times in the world of technology. He's a calm, reassuring voice that recognizes how much EQ is needed in the workplace to foster a positive culture and to allow employees to perform at their best: "What I realize more than ever now is that my job is curation of our culture. If you don't focus on creating a culture that allows people to do their best work, then you've created nothing."[30]

In early 2017, Nadella faced a PR disaster when a new artificial intelligence bot was hacked. Instead of doing its job of bonding humans with AI communication, it said racist, awful things that embarrassed Microsoft. Other leaders might have done everything they could to hide from this; instead, Nadella issued a public apology and used this rift to motivate and inspire his team through empathy and understanding. He said in its aftermath, "It's so critical for leaders not to freak people out, but to give them air cover to solve the real problem. If people are doing things out of fear, it's hard or impossible to actually drive any innovation."[31]

Nadella's leadership has continued to solidify Microsoft's place as one of the most profitable companies in the world. Not long after taking over as CEO, he wanted to put some of his personal touch on the Microsoft mission, so he updated it to read, "Our mission is to empower every person and organization on the planet to achieve more."[32] Talk about a people-first approach! Satya Nadella demonstrates poise, self-awareness, and empathy in one of the most important corporate leadership positions. His mission for Microsoft will endure and leave a lasting impact, and he's helping pave the way by showing his own very high emotional intelligence. As Nadella says, "In the long run, EQ trumps IQ. Without being a source of energy for others, very little can be accomplished."[33]

Poor Leadership

As we swing the pendulum to what poor leadership looks like, you probably have a good visual of exactly what this comprises. We've all experienced micromanaging bosses and leaders who are poor communicators. In these situations, everyone suffers. Getting more specific, here are some hallmark examples of poor leadership:

- Lack of accountability
- "I" before "We," which usually forms a smashing cocktail with "Taking all the credit for something that wasn't his/her own idea or work product"
- Negative attitude and operating from a position of fear
- Overbearing and exerting far too much control in situations where it's unnecessary
- Closed to feedback; cynical mind-set focused only on bottom-line results
- No investment in employees' personal and professional development

We remember the infamous case of Michael Brown, former administrator of the Federal Emergency Management Agency (FEMA) during Hurricane Katrina, whose slow response affected the lives of thousands of citizens. Brown was in charge of the federal government's response to what happened in New Orleans and on the Gulf Coast. He was unprepared, indecisive, and lacked the wherewithal to mobilize people to help rescue and provide aid to those who were struggling to survive.

Remember Kay Whitmore of Eastman Kodak, who didn't evolve with the times in the early 1990s as photography became more digital? His background and experience had been in film, and as technology changed, Whitmore simply didn't recognize or react to the new frontier his industry was entering. Even more baffling, Eastman Kodak had actually developed the first digital camera several years earlier.[34] When he should have been at the forefront of ushering in a new era in photography, Whitmore's inability to proactively respond cost Kodak dearly. It doesn't help his legacy that he ordered the layoffs of more than 10,000 employees to try to keep up with massive losses in profit.[35]

(continued)

What we see in these examples is a lack of adaptability, social skill, and self-awareness. In Brown's case, Katrina was a time for situational leadership; he would have been wise to exercise both the democratic and command style of leadership, but he was ill-prepared and not up for the task. Whitmore couldn't adapt to change, and as a result one of America's leading companies faltered terribly. As recently as 1995, Kodak was a Fortune 50 company; now they are not even a Fortune 500 company. That is the impact of an inability to see and adapt to change.

Most leaders would tell you that it's always important to represent an organization with an upbeat outlook and a passion for the brand. When that's not present, we're often left to wonder about the quality of leadership—or lack thereof. Inspirational and motivational leadership must be backed with substance, an ability to connect with employees, and an ability to stand up in the face of adversity and make intelligent decisions.

No matter where you find yourself in your career, when faced with poor leadership, you can always manage-up in your organization more effectively. Provide feedback and communicate your need for help, but be willing to dive in and solve problems yourself. The initiative and drive to act on your part will improve a culture where poor leadership exists. Be the person who leads both by example and through the power of words.

Democratic

Every great democratic leader will tell you that the secret to their leadership success is building powerful, personalized relationships that translate to collaborative teams. At the heart of democratic leadership is a great listening ear and a mind-set of teamwork, which create the expectation and promulgation of communication and new ideas from employees. Democratic leaders aren't at all inferior to those who are more visionary; quite the opposite. In fact, democratic leaders would probably agree with the famous line from the poem "The Law of the Jungle" by Rudyard Kipling: "For the strength of the pack is the wolf, and the strength of the wolf is the pack."

Democratic leaders perpetually operate in a reciprocal relationship: They inspire and make the people around them better, and they're inspired and made better by the people around them. Their success hinges on the input and valuable contributions of their team, which often pushes them to bigger, bolder frontiers. They excel when they lead by helping their employees discover the best inside themselves. Great listening is at the heart of a truly emotionally intelligent leader. Being open-minded and willing to hear what employees have to say opens up new possibilities for ideas, collaboration, and buy-in, and that leads to new opportunities.

An exemplary model of democratic leadership is the incredibly successful CEO of Stitch Fix, Katrina Lake. In 2017 she became the youngest woman founder ever to lead an IPO.[36] Today her company is worth approximately $2.8 billion, and in 2018 brought in revenue of $1.2 billion. She started the company while attending Harvard for her MBA degree. The Stitch Fix mission is "to change the way people find clothes they love by combining technology with the personal touch of seasoned style experts."[37]

At the heart of the company's operating model is this personal touch of connecting with customers. What has made Katrina Lake's company so successful is her ability to first make this magic happen with her employees: "At Stitch Fix, we encourage our managers to work closely with people and understand how they're feeling about their development and their work . . . we want to make sure that people feel like they're being challenged, that they're learning every day and that they enjoy the people they are spending time with. And I think it's such an important part."[38]

Lake saw that people desire a personal touch in the marketplace. They don't want to be told what to do, but rather to form a partnership. This is also true for team leadership; people want to know they're a part of the process, and whenever possible, it's well worth the investment for democratic leaders to get their employees involved. Think about it: You hire the best people for a reason, not for them to be told what to do but rather to include them, inspire them, and encourage them to lift their voices and be involved.

A potential downside of democratic leadership is having too many people involved in the decision-making process, thus leading to delays. When quick, timely decisions are required, it's best not to involve too many people. This leadership style might also lead to complacency if employees feel that the leader isn't enough of an authority figure. We see democratic leadership more these days in flat organizational structures, but it still works best when there is a clear decision-maker who can move swiftly when required.

Democratic leaders are self-aware enough to recognize that their brand is simply the outward representation of their culture. To have a great external appearance, you need to empower the people on the inside to contribute, have a voice, and add value each day while knowing they are valued.

Relationships are at the heart of business at all levels. One of the ways I began to grow as a businessman was by joining a "mastermind" group of fellow writers and coaches who pushed me and stoked the fire of my curiosity. I gained valuable ideas, but it was the relationships I built that opened my mind to the type of professional I really wanted to be. These individuals expanded my audience and helped my ideas connect with a new community of people who never would have heard them otherwise.

To succeed as leaders, to reach the masses and expand into territories we never imagined, we have to do the powerful work of building life-changing relationships. Start by being a great listener and get valuable input from those you lead. As Dr. Guy Itzchakov and Avraham Kluger write in the *Harvard Business Review*: "Listening resembles a muscle. It requires training, persistence, effort, and most importantly, the intention to become a good listener. It requires clearing your mind from internal and external noise—and if this isn't possible, postponing a conversation for when you can truly listen without being distracted."[39]

Surround yourself with other winners who encourage you, support you, and build you up. Empathy is intrinsically self-giving and generous in nature. It's not selfish. It's not self-seeking and motivated by "What's in it for me?" thinking. Successful leaders know that leading and serving others with an empathetic, service-minded approach yields higher returns and dividends than seeking only to benefit ourselves.

Listen with deep presence and attention. There is remarkable power in listening with intent and concern to what someone else has to say. They appreciate you more and you process valuable information more clearly. As Dr. Stephen Covey once said, "It's a win-win."

Pacesetting

Pacesetting leaders play an up-tempo game at all times and expect their employees to rise to the standard of performance and level of competition. Pacesetters thrive on competition, both with themselves and also with internal and external sources. It's clear to their followers that pacesetting leaders have ambition, drive, and a tremendous will to succeed; there's no shortage of intrinsic motivation. At their best, pacesetting leaders inspire creativity and get their employees to perform at their highest level while also taking the time to explain the purpose behind what they're doing. The danger to the organization is when they become too competitive and the organization operates in overdrive for an extended period of time.

Great pacesetting leadership is exemplified by leaders who set the standard very high and lead both through words and by example to lift other members of the organization to their level. They supply the necessary tools and inspire others to figure out how to work together to achieve goals. In the early part of her career, Sara Blakely was a high-achieving pacesetting leader. She put in extraordinarily long hours and worked to the point of exhaustion. She was practically the entire C-suite herself: the CEO, CMO, COO, etc. As Spanx began to grow in

2000, she recruited friends to work from her apartment to fill orders. She couldn't do it all, so she found help anywhere she could get it to push forward and drive growth.

As she gained more partners on the supplier and customer sides, she was able to add new employees and spend more time marketing her product. She shifted back into being a visionary leader, creating markets where they hadn't existed.

Pacesetting leaders excel when they're paired with high-performing teams comprised of talented individuals who don't mind the challenge of working in high-pressure environments. Think about the times you've found yourself in a pressure cooker, working for a boss who seemed to relentlessly ask for more, in less time, and at the same budget. It's difficult, to say the least, but the rewards are high when your output matches the outsized expectations of the leader. In today's world of employees being asked to wear multiple hats, it's not uncommon to see leaders and their direct reports doing the jobs of several people. Pacesetting leaders are best served by acknowledging these conditions, showing empathy, and offering positive, motivating feedback to show how they appreciate their teams.

The many modern organizations operating under these circumstances welcome a pacesetting leader who understands this nuance and can blend their business acumen and work ethic with an emotionally intelligent mind-set. Problems can arise when these social skills aren't present, and the cost to an organization in turnover can be huge.

A stellar example of a pacesetting leader is Richard Branson, who said, "My number one rule in business, and in life, is to enjoy what you do. Running a business involves long hours and hard decisions; if you don't have the passion to keep you going, your business will more than likely fail." Branson's many successes have also come with some spectacular failures. But let me ask you this—what do you most remember him for? It's probably not for Virgin Cola or Virgin Brides! Rather, his estimated $5 billion fortune came from Virgin Mobile, Virgin Records, and his many other successful business ventures. It's because he kept driving forward and demanding a higher standard from his employees that he is the highly successful leader we know today. He talks regularly about how work needs to be fun and how the bonding of teams is essential, but he's also known as one of the hardest workers around. Like Sara Blakely, he is a visionary business leader whose work ethic helped drive him to success. He earned the respect of the people who work for him because he listens with empathy and has a self-improving mind-set that prizes continuous learning.

Take Branson's perspective on how he fortified his mind-set into becoming an incredible winner in business: "My mother drummed into me from an early age that I should not spend much time regretting the past. I try to bring that discipline to my business career. Over the years, my team and I have not let mistakes, failures or mishaps get us down. Instead, even when a venture has failed, we try to look for opportunities, to see whether we can capitalize on another gap in the market."[40]

Pacesetting leaders can lose trust and connection with their employees in the long term if they're always sprinting. Leadership is a marathon, and it's detrimental to drive people hard all the time. When it's always "busy" season, employees can experience burnout and become disillusioned. Stories of overwork in the financial world are common, and we see this with technology companies, too. Brilliant leaders in tech set ambitious goals. With those goals can come very long hours and the expectation that an employee take on several roles at once. In the short term, the pacesetting style has its benefits. In the long term, however, it can fracture relationships and sour the culture as employees look elsewhere for a better work-life balance.

Commanding

When asked to think of a traditional leader, people often think of commanding leaders. These leaders have ambitious goals and are competitive, driven, and assertive. For commanding leaders, emotional intelligence is beneficial in understanding the nuance of a situation. Self-awareness is paramount here to avoid lingering too long in the commanding style. While it's important to push hard for results, leaders must exercise self-control to avoid pushing people too far over the edge. One effective way to balance the commanding style with an emotionally intelligent approach is for leaders to explain themselves in an empathetic way to individuals, perhaps after addressing a group as a whole.

As a prime example, consider a VP of sales running a sales organization. She/he might address the group as a whole in a stern, commanding voice to let everyone know that they must meet their sales metrics by the end of the quarter or everyone may be out of a job. In private, the leader might meet individually with trusted sales people to allay their fears by telling them she/he cares about them and recognizes this is a tough time. An even better approach would be for the leader to relay an anecdote from a time when she/he was in this position before—and came out on top.

There's simply no denying that this type of leadership can be effective when executed in an authentic, self-aware way. Take, for example, a military unit on a reconnaissance mission where lives are at stake each minute. In a top-down environment like the military, this type of leadership is respected and valued. Clear direction and certitude in approach help provide clarity and, at their best, can remove any doubts or concerns about the mission.

A command leadership style is meant for unique situations like crises and emergencies. The problem with a commanding leader is that eventually people will learn to fear and not respect this person. Employees eventually tune out leaders who sustain a commanding "Do what I tell you" style. Fear drives their influence, and trust is breached when employees lose respect. It's extraordinarily difficult for any leader to regain trust.

The commanding style is best suited for situations in which a leader is thrust into an extremely difficult set of circumstances. Leaders who place high demands on the people they lead, and even raise their voice or challenge them publicly to meet metrics of performance, are best served by having already built a relationship on common values.

It's important to remember that a commanding style of leadership isn't all bad. Think about how helpful a commanding style would have been in sports organizations like USA Gymnastics and FIFA, both of which have suffered from embarrassing scandals of failed leadership. And in the finance world—from the 2008 subprime mortgage crisis to the scandals that badly affected Wells Fargo and Bank of America—there has been a jarring lack of accountability. At its best, a commanding leadership style is direct, transparent, and one where the leader takes ownership and accountability.

When we feel a commanding style is needed, we must make sure to understand the ramifications that can come from it. We risk alienating people, especially those in our inner circle. We risk attrition—watching our best people leave. The benefits involve getting people to mobilize quickly, and with expedited action, but this leadership style works best when combined with a keen self-awareness and mindful approach of empathy. Yes, you can be both commanding and empathetic. A great model of this balance is one of the most revered American military figures in modern history, General Colin Powell, who said, "Leaders must embed their own sense of purpose into the heart and soul of every follower. The purpose starts from the leader at the top, and through infectious, dynamic, passionate leadership, it is driven down through the organization."[41]

Colin Powell proudly served his country as national security advisor, chairman of the joint chiefs of staff, and secretary of state, among many other prestigious positions. To say Colin Powell was a respected leader would be like saying Oprah Winfrey built a successful business. Powell succeeded during his time in the military with a commanding style that was also deeply personal.

Both as a military leader and as a politician in the highest ranks of the federal government, Powell seemed to perpetually live in high-pressure situations that demanded tough decisions and authority. As he matured as a public servant, he grew as a situational leader who adapted to his surroundings and displayed magnificent cognizance of decision-making for each key moment. "To achieve his purpose, a successful leader must set demanding standards and make sure they are met. Followers want to be 'in a good outfit,' as we say in the Army. I never saw a good unit that wasn't always stretching to meet a higher standard . . . Standards must be achievable and the leaders must provide the means to get there."[42]

In summation, commanding leaders are great when the situation requires authoritative leadership, control, and clear communication and direction. The risks of this style include a negative effect on employees' emotions, the absence of room for debate, a "my way or the highway" attitude, and the risk of losing respect and trust. Commanding leaders must be mindful of long-term repercussions to the organization; it is here, especially, where a high degree of self-awareness is required to be effective.

Your Leadership Style

Take this five-question assessment to determine your leadership style.

1. Consider the style of leadership you actually use in your job, and then rank the six styles of leadership in descending order of importance for you (visionary, coaching, affiliative, democratic, pacesetting, and commanding). What are your thoughts looking at your rank-ordered list?
2. What leadership style do you currently use that you feel is **most** to your advantage?
3. What leadership style do you not use as much that you think could help you most? List particular situations you face to help clarify your thoughts.
4. List three positive and three negative attributes for each leadership style as they specifically pertain to your role in your current organization. How can you integrate (and eliminate) styles to become a more emotionally intelligent leader?
5. What leadership style would you most frequently like to experience? The beauty of leadership styles is that they are situational (we'll talk later about situational leadership), but usually leaders predominantly exhibit one style over others. Think about all six and determine, for your own style and personality, which you'd most like to work with.

Keeping in mind the five pillars of EQ—self-awareness, self-management, motivation, empathy, and social skill—this assessment is truly an exercise in self-awareness and social skill. To experience leadership, you have to immerse yourself in it as the practitioner and as the "end user." Give this some clear, focused thought. This exercise could go a long way toward reaffirming, or perhaps shaping, your leadership style.

Takeaways

No matter the leadership style you choose to adopt in a given situation, take the time to invest in the people you lead. The time to do that is always now. Great leaders are remembered for their business successes and profits, to be sure, but they're also remembered for the way they treated the people around them. As we saw in the story of Katrina Lake, she built a highly profitable company by always putting the development needs of her employees first.

Lynda Weinman built an online learning empire by having the self-awareness and adaptability to create courses in web design—and beyond—that were evolving at the speed of technology, beginning with an understanding of what people really needed.

There is room for all kinds of successful leaders. Visionary, coaching, affiliative, democratic, pacesetting, and commanding styles all have their benefits, and some their drawbacks. Study the descriptions and determine which one most suits your personality. And remember: You can always adapt and approach each situation in the way that will serve your team and organization best.

CHAPTER FOUR

Becoming an Emotionally Intelligent Leader

We have the power when it comes to emotional intelligence. That is the most important part of understanding how to use it to our advantage. We can all increase and improve our EQ.

If you are just starting out, in this chapter you'll find foundational activities like goal-setting, making time for personal development, and reflection for getting to know yourself better. For more experienced leaders at more senior levels, the transforming section is for you. This is where you continue to assess, take inventory of your skills, and determine how to refine them. In this phase, you build relationships that take your career to new heights.

Empathy may not come naturally to us in the workplace, but it may be exactly what our employees need and are asking for. This chapter details the catalysts for change and describes how to get going, and then discusses ways to resist regressive behavior and how to reinvent ourselves. We all have the ability to lock in what we gain and continue growing into the leader we want to be.

First Steps

Are you willing to do the hard work of getting to know yourself more deeply than you ever have?

Are you prepared to ask yourself the tough questions and answer them with clear eyes?

Are you going to go after what you really want, even if it feels uncomfortable?

I start with these three questions because the answers are essential to increasing your emotional intelligence. If you're serious about boosting your EQ and becoming a sought-after thought leader, you have to focus first and foremost on yourself. Chapter 2, on the pillars of emotionally intelligent leadership, started with self-awareness for a reason. It all begins with self-awareness, with knowing who you really are. As you'll see in the first activity at the close of this chapter, I give you five ways to start.

The work begins, as we've previously discussed, by spending time on yourself first. If you're going to lead others effectively, you need to have your own house in order. In the executive coaching work I do, I talk about having a solid structure in place. I call this the "EQ Game Plan for Leaders." As we discussed in chapter 2 on self-awareness, this means having clarity around your values, passion, purpose, mission, and goals. When you're clear on these things, you build the self-confidence and motivation to grow into the vision of yourself you've imagined. In the same way that great companies have a vision, purpose, and mission, we can personalize these things for ourselves.

While your game plan will be relatively concise, it's a lot harder to complete than you think. It requires that you get honest about your true self. To get to your authentic core as a person and leader, you need to hold yourself to a high standard with commitment and discipline. It's here that you can begin to build the foundation for your life and career. Once you have your structure in place, you begin by doing some reverse engineering. Start with the results, not only in mind, but in writing! Write down exactly what you want to achieve—the results that you're willing to work so hard for. From there, build backward to create exactly what you want.

Shifting to a longer-term strategy, I'm a major proponent of putting together a five-year plan for your life. I've heard this wisdom from Fortune 500 executives, CEOs, retired millionaires, and respected friends. I've heard it so often, and from so many people I admire, that it's become one of most important building blocks I believe a leader should have.

There's an astonishing power that takes hold in your life when you speak and write down your dreams. You simply need to will yourself to do it. It honestly *is* that simple, but it's not so easy to sit down to do it. Any plan is only worth the self-sacrifice and commitment to action you're willing to make. The best plans in the world are nothing if you're not willing to act. Know this: You will need to adjust your plan. You must keep going and make adjustments as life changes all around you. That's the secret of change and the secret of life. You truly can achieve your dreams if you're willing to plan and act on them.

One of the great models in life, the late coach John Wooden, defined success as "peace of mind, which is a direct result of self-satisfaction in knowing you made the effort to become the best you are capable of becoming."[43]

Success is an *attitude* and requires maximum effort. It is peace of mind and a state of mind. And please note the emphasis on *self* in self-satisfaction. Your success should never be determined by the approval or recognition of others. If so, you'll live a highly disappointing life. As you begin each day, I implore you to ask yourself, "What will success look like today?" Answering this question is one of the first steps you should take when looking to grow into a better leader.

As you begin to put your plan together, visualization gets your juices flowing and makes you hunger to achieve your goal. Visualization and imagination go hand in hand to kindle the fire inside that fuels your motivation and determination. There is power in reciting your plan out loud.

Last but not least, mix faith with your written and spoken words to fuse them together. The rest is all about executing your plan. You need courage and energy to propel yourself forward and never look back, and this comes from believing you're on the right path.

Another great first step to take is a philosophical one. It is extremely helpful to have a philosophy around what you hope to be and what you intend to accomplish. Some people call this a personal creed; I call it your personal mission statement. This is written documentation that establishes three things:

1. Your why

2. Your direction

3. The substance of things that matter to you

Your purpose—or your *raison d'être*—is the reason you're doing what you're doing. This should be organic and developed only by you, free from any influences or emotions of the moment.

Your direction determines the actions you must take in order to fulfill the requirements of your *why*. Too often, new leaders doubt themselves because they don't think they're *ready* to begin moving in the direction of what they want to accomplish. They think it's not their time, that they're lacking in a particular area, or that they're too young. They're hindered by limiting beliefs that beget doubt and fear.

It may make sense to begin with very tiny steps toward completing tasks and goals that match up with your purpose. This is where writing out your goals and putting them into a plan comes in. This is your direction, the compass that will guide you when life gets in the way, when you're too busy or too tired. Planning is essential.

The substance of things that matter to you are part and parcel of your *why*, and should be incorporated, as much as possible, into what you do each day. These are the core values, ideals, principles, people, and things that bring enthusiasm and passion to your life.

Now you can write your clear, succinct mission statement. Here is mine: *To help others and make a tangible difference in their lives through my writing, speaking, and coaching, while living each moment to the fullest, and having a positive attitude, smile, and genuine enjoyment for life.*

Values give us a strong core from which to navigate the peaks and valleys we'll encounter. Some values that leaders assimilate into their arsenal include honesty, confidence, perseverance, kindness, and humility. These are universally accepted and beneficial values and key components to leadership, no matter the venue.

If you asked Steve Jobs what made him great, he would have told you intelligent direction, belief in himself, hard work, and enthusiasm and passion. It's why one of his famous quotes—from an all-time epic speech—is an exhortation to follow your heart. Values matter to successful businessmen and women, and to you and me.

Hold yourself to weekly accountability checks. Carve out 30 minutes of quiet time on a day that you know you will be able to focus. Review your mission statement. Review your goals. Are you achieving them? If not, what could you do differently? Remember: It's not always about adding in new things; sometimes it's equally as important to remove tasks and activities that aren't adding value. These first steps provide a solid start for the structure you'll need to take big steps forward as an emotionally intelligent leader.

First Steps Exercise: Mission Statement

Here's how to set up yours:

1. Your *why*: Why are you doing what you're doing? Who are you doing it for? Dig deep and ask yourself reflective questions, like *what is this leading me toward*? Crystal-clear awareness of your thoughts will inform your actions.
2. Your direction: What steps do you need to take to get where you really want to be? Write these out. These become success measures that will hold you accountable and inspire you.
3. List everything in your life that matters to you, and go deeper. Why do these things matter to you? How do they resonate with you? How do they touch you in a meaningful way and make you think, "I have to have these in my life"?

With clarity on all three elements, you can write out your succinct, personal mission statement. If you'd like, use mine from this chapter as an example.

First Steps Exercise: Build Your EQ Game Plan

You saw this one coming, didn't you!

1. What do you want? Everything begins with this fundamental question.
2. List your values (e.g., faith, honesty, integrity, perseverance, humility).
3. List your passions. These motivating factors will light the fire inside you. Don't focus only on work items; you can include personal items as well.
4. Purpose—why are you doing what you're doing?

5. Mission—how will you define success?
6. Goals—what specific, measurable outcomes are you trying to achieve?

You have your game plan. Just like the foundation of a house, your structure is now in place. To bridge the gap from planning to execution, start plotting out the tasks that you need to complete in order to reach your goals. Manage those on your digital or analog schedule, and commit!

First Steps Exercise: Five-Year Plan

What would you most like to accomplish professionally in the next five years? Use these questions to help guide you:

- What professional development courses would you like to take, what conferences would you like to attend, or what certifications would you like to obtain?

- In 100 words, describe the job you'd love to have that meshes with your talents, knowledge, skills, experiences, and passion.

- List all your business skills. Then list your transferable skills to see how they translate to another industry or business venture; e.g., public speaking could translate into a variety of leadership roles.

Transforming

The best leadership advice I've ever received is very simple: Start building relationships right away. I mean both the relationship you have with yourself, and the relationships you build in your personal and professional life. In First Steps, we mostly discussed the relationship with yourself. In order to give value to others in your organization, you must first introspectively look within and be firm in your values, strategy, and goals. The transforming leader masters the fundamentals of self-awareness and then builds relationships with people both inside and outside their organization. The transforming leader knows that driving change and action requires building relational capital and doing so with empathy and an authentic desire to elevate others.

Relationships are the turbocharger that lead to new opportunities, success, and the achievement of our long-term goals. No matter how introverted, individualistic, or innovative we are, we cannot make it on our own. Think about it: How often do we scramble to make things work without having built a relationship with people? And how often does that work out? To mobilize people and move them toward achieving strategic goals, transformative leaders should always be in the mind-set of getting to know their employees. Authentic business relationships are built on curiosity, candor, and a willingness to help.

Forging relationships helps increase our mental inventory of knowledge. We learn what will work in this environment and what won't. We gather knowledge on organizational politics, leadership, and history. So much of what defines success at a job is learning the company history, finding what makes people tick, and showing a genuine desire to help.

The time to build these vitally important work relationships is day one! Relationships collect serious compound interest over time, so it's best to begin early. Whether you're at a startup, hedge fund, food services company, or ad agency, you will benefit exponentially from building powerful relationships that are real, authentic, and genuine. If you're just doing it to climb the ladder or "game the system," people will sniff the phoniness a mile away, and they won't want to help.

Transformational leaders are astutely aware of the needs of their employees, and are wise to modify their leadership styles depending on the situation. Situational Leadership,[44] the brainchild of the late

Dr. Paul Hersey and Ken Blanchard, author of the bestselling book *The One-Minute Manager*, lays out a framework for how to approach leadership in each situation, depending on the readiness of the employees you're dealing with. Situational leadership is truly about adaptability. It's rooted in change! Given the vicissitudes of the market and the constantly evolving business landscape, this framework—rooted in years of research—is trusted by so many businesses. It teaches you how to lead depending on the readiness level of your employees.

Employees want to be recognized by their leadership. They want to feel a sense of belonging, particularly one that is reflected in the culture. They want to know more about their leaders both as decision-makers and human beings. Dr. Andrew Chamberlain, chief economist for Glassdoor, has the research to back this up: "Across all income levels, the top predictor of workplace satisfaction is *not* pay: It is the culture and values of the organization, followed closely by the quality of senior leadership and the career opportunities at the company. Among the six workplace factors examined, compensation and benefits were consistently rated among the *least* important factors of workplace happiness."[45]

A transformational leader recognizes that company values and culture will determine the success of their organization. They develop a structure that is more of a meritocracy, rewarding top performers and providing them with the upward mobility needed to one day get into senior leadership positions. They listen to the needs of their employees, working with team leaders to adapt performance management and putting the *human* element into human resources to ensure that good people stay around. Dr. Michael D. Watkins, renowned expert on transitions in business, said, "To be successful, you need to mobilize the energy of many others in your organization. If you do the right things, then your vision, your expertise, and your drive can propel you forward and serve as seed crystals."[46]

As we learned from the story of transformative leader Richard Branson in chapter 3, adversity is not our enemy! Look back at your life and ask yourself, "How did I respond in the face of difficulty, adversity, or loss?" You'll learn a lot about yourself and you'll make your greatest strides once you begin to use adversity to your advantage.

A transformative leader is also a change catalyst with the ability to foresee change and adjust before it happens. As we learned, Payal Kadakia understood the changing attitudes of consumers when it came to personal fitness. Struggling to find classes she wanted, she suspected and learned that others felt the same way. By providing a service that was in demand but not previously offered, Kadakia's vision demonstrated that if she built it, they would come.

This is work we all can accomplish on our own once we determine the most important things in our work roles—or as I like to call them, *the big rocks*. The big rocks are things like achieving the goals in your strategic plan, developing new leaders, hitting revenue markers, and ensuring you have the right people in the right positions. Transformative leaders focus on the most important things and delegate the pebbles to other members of the team.

It's hard to talk about transforming without discussing reinvention. Transforming leaders are never content—and certainly not complacent—with the success they've achieved in their careers. They know that personal development (e.g., coaching, meditation, reading new books) and professional development (e.g., attending leadership conferences, learning a new technology, training) are essential for them to continue furthering their leadership capabilities. A transforming leader seeks feedback (or, as we'll discuss in the next session, "feedforward"), which helps them gauge their progress. A transforming leader aims to improve both strengths and weaknesses. All around, transforming leaders are mindful, self-aware, and motivated to make each day their masterpiece as they continue to develop new ways to move their organization forward.

Transforming Exercise: Game Plan for Leaders Assessment

Head over to my website, http://chrisdconnors.com, and take the EQ Game Plan for Leaders Assessment under the Tools section. There you'll find 10 questions that cover the range of emotional intelligence qualities. This will help you assess how you're currently performing and, based on your results, will provide areas of focus to help you increase your emotional intelligence.

Transforming Exercise: Evolution

Here are five questions to ask yourself as you evolve into an emotionally intelligent leader:

1. What is the cost to me of staying in the same spot and *not* changing?
2. What behaviors have *not* worked for me in the past? What did I learn from them?
3. What do I see as my biggest leadership need?
4. What leader can I learn about and emulate to continue my progression into becoming the leader that I want to be?
5. What are the best "quick wins" (based on the five pillars of EQ: self-awareness, self-management, motivation, empathy, and social skill) that I can immediately begin to assimilate into my thoughts, words, and actions?

Transforming Exercise: Facing Adversity

What are the three most difficult experiences you've ever dealt with as a leader (personally or professionally)?

Write what it felt like when they first occurred, and then write what you did in the aftermath to recover mentally and emotionally. Next, list the lessons you learned from each of these instances. What qualities and traits of EQ did you exhibit while going through your biggest moments of adversity? How are you better today for that adversity, and how has it made you a stronger leader?

Common Challenges

A very common challenge for anyone becoming an emotionally intelligent leader is overcoming the perception that people will take advantage when you lead with empathy. Some people think "putting people first" is code for "people will march all over you." You may have an image of a leader who is dominant, less personable, and too focused on the bottom line to make time for conversation. Sadly, depending on the industry, stereotypical leaders like this can exist.

Being an emotionally intelligent leader is far from a sign of weakness; rather, it's a strength that unites the organization. As Simon Sinek artfully says in *Leaders Eat Last*, "When a leader embraces their responsibility to care for people instead of caring for numbers, then people will follow, solve problems and see to it that that leader's vision comes to life the right way, a stable way and not the expedient way."[47]

Another common challenge facing emotionally intelligent leaders is revealing more of themselves personally to the people they lead. For leaders who are private by nature, this isn't easy. It can be a challenge to open up about your true self. If you're more introverted, it can be hard to find the motivation for social time. See this social time as an opportunity to *connect* and share yourself with others, rather than an event that enervates you. As your employees see more of the authentic you, it will help strip away fear and let you connect with confidence.

If you've succeeded as a leader without evolving your style or trying on new roles, chances are you'll struggle at first. What if you're suddenly asked to head a new department where you lack subject matter experience, but you're trusted because of your business acumen? How are you going to adapt to learning something new, working with new teams, and perhaps leaning on others more than you have before?

Given how frequently roles change—and let's be honest, some of us change organizations every couple of years—it's important to have an agile mind-set. It's all too common for a leader to be moved from one business unit to another and feel totally lost. Immerse yourself by understanding other departmental functions and learning about each organizational leadership role. By having a working knowledge of that team's core functions and, of course, having built key relationships in your new department, promotional opportunities can develop.

Too many leaders think they only need to know one discipline; that's outdated thinking. Become the expert in one area, but "diversify your portfolio" by growing your knowledge in multiple business functions. It's a win-win for company knowledge and the growth of key relationships. Get comfortable with being uncomfortable. Challenge yourself in ways you haven't before.

Being agile and responsive to the needs of the business, having a balanced team, and knowing how to best employ your strengths while compensating for your weaknesses are signs of a truly adaptable, high-EQ leader.

Resisting Regression

It's a lot easier to fall back into a bad habit than it is to stay the course with a good one. As an emotionally intelligent leader, we know that we have the power within us to grow and improve. We also know that it's not easy. It takes time, discipline, and work. Unfortunately, for many of us, some of the basics of EQ don't come naturally. They require our attention and awareness at all times. The best productivity and time-management guidance instructs us to form habits, which in and of itself implicitly urges us to practice consistency and commitment. So it's here in this disciplined mind-set that we must operate if we're to avoid regressive behavior, such as:

- Forgetting everything we know to be right because the pressure of the moment causes us to act in desperation

- Making a firing or promoting decision on a whim

- Giving ourselves all the credit and none of the blame

- Stubbornly thinking we can lead by decree, raised voice, or demand, particularly when it's not an emergency situation

- Eliminating time for reflection and building up our core selves because "we've advanced beyond that fundamental stage"

Regressive behavior shows deficiency in all the core components of emotional intelligence. You're downgrading from the improvements you've made because stress, change, pressure, and circumstances have rattled you. Rather than turning back to the foundation you've built, you've resorted to short-term thinking. Short-term thinking prioritizes tactics over strategy. We're always most successful when we have a strategy behind what we do. This requires thought, mindfulness, and an evaluation of pros and cons. Emotionally intelligent leaders make the conscious choice to behave the way they do.

Acting with empathy doesn't come naturally to everyone, and as a result it can be the first thing that goes as we become self-centered. Tough breaks, dips in the market, or a loss to a competitor can slow the motivation of even the most self-inspired leaders. Decisions are either delayed or made haphazardly without a purpose behind them. Always remember, high-EQ leaders show empathy toward themselves.

I hope you are always compassionate to yourself, both privately and publicly. Despite the winds of change and emotion, it's imperative to find time to be kind to ourselves. This is where surrounding ourselves with people who love and empathize with us matters so much. We must always stay true to ourselves. Privately, I know you have pride and an ego. So do I. So does everyone! We mustn't ever let our perception of how people see us change the way we carry ourselves. Over the long haul, life will be so much better if we lead with integrity.

The quality that people respect most is persistence. As an emotionally intelligent leader, this persistence—drive—is what enables us to take the first step and keep going. There's an art to persistent communication. There's a talent in being persistent and working toward our goals every day. In fact, I'd rather be known for my persistence, perseverance, attitude, and work ethic than my talents. Maybe you would, as well.

We can have all the talent in the world, but if we're not working hard and being persistent every day, it won't matter. No matter where you are in your career, ask yourself, "Can I give more each day to becoming the best version of myself that I can?" I think you'll find the answer is yes. People will respect you for it.

As discussed in chapter 2, the best way to thwart regressive behavior is with a fully self-aware mind-set toward addition and subtraction. I like to call it playing offense and defense. Most of us spend our time squarely in the offensive zone. We look for every advantage. We try new strategies toward achieving the same outcomes. We take courses to learn something new. We network and try to build new relationships. These are all great things with a high value assigned to them.

The problem is that if this isn't accompanied by a defensive mind-set—one that also focuses on eliminating time-wasters and self-destructive thinking, behavior, and activities—then all the high-value activities won't matter. Emotionally intelligent people are successful because they learn about themselves, recognize their thoughts, behaviors, and actions, and then adapt and modify their behaviors to focus on high-value activities. They eliminate tasks and activities that either add no value or take them down a notch. These are high-value, "playing offense" activities:

- Spending time each day in meditation (and prayer, depending on your spiritual preferences)

- Keeping a journal for self-reflection to express your thoughts, feelings, and emotions, both personally and professionally

- Thinking of the people in your everyday interactions that you can help—meeting them for lunch or coffee and simply asking, "How can I help you?"

- Planning and organizing your time blocks each week for meetings, idea creation, and work you need to focus on

- Beginning your day with, and seeding in moments for, inspirational reading and videos

- Visualizing yourself achieving your exact goals and definition of success, imagining what that looks like, how it makes you feel, and what it will take for you to get to that moment

These are "playing defense" activities:

- Examining how you spend time in your day and identifying things that aren't helpful

- Determining what meetings and tasks you can delegate

- Building in contingency time for inevitable emergencies or circumstances that demand your attention

We must be mindful of the words we say, the thoughts that enter our mind, and the things we write. Make a habit of cutting out excuses. Excuses lead to a lack of ownership, which is the mark of someone who is off-loading responsibility onto others. Eliminate excuses because they lead to procrastination. By putting off things we don't want to do, the most likely outcome is that we end up criticizing ourselves, regretting our wasted time, and, in the worst case, we lose sleep and experience higher stress levels. Putting off things that demand our attention now is not a winning proposition.

To help address regressive behavior, take this "feedforward" approach from famed coach Marshall Goldsmith, via the *Harvard Business Review*:

1. Describe your goal clearly and simply to anyone you know.

2. Ask for two suggestions. Encourage creative ideas.

3. Listen carefully. Write the suggestions down.

4. Respond with "thank you." Nothing more. No excuses or defensiveness.

5. Repeat by asking additional people.[48]

Embracing a constantly self-improving mind-set will combat any types of regressive behavior that may enter your mind. The "feedforward" part is about accepting suggestions and asking for as much help in that area as you can to help you grow. Be proactive and remain open as you make big strides as a leader.

Resisting Regression Exercise: Process of Elimination

Create a list of personal and professional things you need to give up to reach a level of wellness and performance you can be proud of. For example, it could be related to your diet, or maybe it's eliminating negative words or phrases from your vocabulary. Perhaps it's simply eliminating excuses.

Break your list into the four areas of wellness: emotional, spiritual, physical, and mental.

What is holding you back from becoming a better leader at home and at work?

Resisting Regression Exercise: System

It's one thing to have a plan, and another to back it up with a system you use to hold yourself accountable.

I love the Bullet Journal as an analog tool to compliment any digital schedule management tools like Gmail, Outlook, etc. For this exercise, I encourage you to commit to a daily practice of listing the following:

- Notes
- Tasks
- Events

Lock in 15 minutes of uninterrupted time to do this at the start of each day. What are the highest-value tasks and events? Build around those and be diligent as you work through each item. Having a system enables you to prioritize each input and to determine what needs to get done, what can be delegated, and what doesn't require your focus.

Resisting Regression Exercise: Weekly Scorecard

Which of the following items did you do this week? Be honest with yourself.

Self-Awareness

- ☐ I reflected on the way I felt each day and kept a brief journal.
- ☐ There was a purpose behind each action I took.

Empathy

- ☐ I listened first and spoke second.
- ☐ I focused my full energy and attention on who I was meeting with.

Motivation

- ☐ I found passion and energy during the course of each day.
- ☐ I inspired the people around me with my words and actions.

Self-Management

- ☐ I had a plan for each day.
- ☐ I recognized moments of adversity, took the time to understand my emotions, and acted in a way I'm proud of.

Social Skill

- ☐ I connected emotionally with team members.
- ☐ I rallied team members around an idea I believe in.

Use this scorecard each week to keep getting better, and challenge yourself in a positive, competitive way to keep raising your score!

Takeaways

If you're taking your first steps, focus on building your game plan and completing a mission statement. Your company builds its foundation on values, defining success, and having a vision, and you can do the same thing for yourself. As you transform and evolve as a leader, please recognize the incredible importance of change. Adapting to a new environment, building new relationships, and doing the introspective work of determining what you need to do to improve will make a world of difference in your professional development. Focus on yourself, and then take the positive strides you've made and build and cultivate relationships where you are. You never know when you'll need them.

Understand what it means to play both offense and defense within your role. To avoid slipping back into bad habits, focus on the high-value activities you can incorporate into your daily routine. Conversely, eliminate negative time-wasters and any unnecessary tasks and meetings on your schedule. Realize how much progress you've made, and be energized by all that's to come.

CHAPTER FIVE

Creating Emotionally Intelligent Organizations

As a leader, you have the ability to build a culture that employees want to be a part of. The goal is to create a dynamic culture that will help you earn "raving fans" in the form of both customers and employees. The insights herein will show you how to do this. Building a winning culture takes empathy, adaptability, a positive outlook, and belief in people. When you express these qualities as a leader, employees will show you the drive and motivation it takes to build and maintain a collaborative, cohesive environment.

We'll present a roadmap for turning your vision into reality for facilitating growth and connection on your team and across business units. Finally, we'll focus on the obstacles to building a healthy, emotionally intelligent organization. You've been equipped with examples of great leaders, leadership styles, and tools for your personal development, and now it's time to leverage those into growing an emotionally intelligent organization.

Culture

Culture is the lifeblood of any organization. Organizations with great cultures never have to worry about reputation. As we saw in the case of Southwest Airlines, the culture at Southwest was so filled with spirit, love, and energy that it grew to represent the brand's reputation both in marketing and in practice. If you've ever flown Southwest, you know the experience is more than just your average flight; it's a rollicking 35,000-feet jaunt with a sense of humor, flair, and panache.

As famous management consultant Peter Drucker once said, "Culture eats strategy for breakfast." Whether you're leading a startup venture, helming an industry-leading organization, or helping a company make the transition from growth phase to expansion, you need to begin by understanding the culture. Emotionally intelligent leaders are passionate about culture because they know winning organizations have a positive, people-first culture. An open culture, one that is receptive and ready for new ideas, is fertile ground for an emotionally intelligent leader.

As we learned in the brilliant story of Satya Nadella at Microsoft, his focus was first on culture, not strategy. Microsoft's top executives were divided, and the company was increasingly siloed. Nadella realized that he needed to introduce empathy and adaptability to survive, but also to shape the way people see one another at Microsoft.

Nadella understood that Microsoft would succeed when its employees communicated more with one another and became more open-minded and welcome to change. He saw that Microsoft wasn't concerned enough about the business of its own people, so his first effort was to learn the perspective of his own employees. With empathy and nuanced social skills, he showed that he wanted to listen. With chief people officer Kathleen Hogan, he started a grassroots effort to change the culture.

Nadella excelled by recognizing that he needed to change things in the present while using his vision, intuition, and business acumen to build a more self-aware workforce for the future. "The reason I talk about empathy is that I believe this is the leading indicator of success. Innovation comes only when you are able to meet unmet, unarticulated needs—and this comes from a deep sense of empathy we all have. But you can't go to work and, say, 'turn on the empathy button.' Your life's experience will give you that passion and understanding for a particular customer, a particular use case."[49]

It's easy to think of the Golden Rule when we discuss building and shaping an emotionally intelligent culture. You're always wise to revisit the core values of respect and integrity. Encourage employees to call out unethical and immoral behavior. Make it known that your team or business unit won't tolerate sexual harassment or discrimination. Likewise, define what it means to be a great team: qualities like camaraderie, "attitude and effort," commitment, and attention to detail. Highlight the outstanding attributes of an excellent teammate.

People First

In a crowd of leaders, one man has stood out throughout the years. If you're unfamiliar with the incredible life story of John Paul DeJoria, the founder of hair care company Paul Mitchell, liquor company Patrón Spirits, and now telecommunications company ROKiT, it's worth understanding how this brilliant man went from being homeless to a multibillionaire. He started out as a door-to-door salesman and later partnered with Paul Mitchell to found the hair care company. He prioritized two things: making the best product, and putting his people first. He's had very minimal turnover at his company over the years—less than 100 employees in nearly 40 years.

He accomplished this by treating his employees with love and kindness. As he said, "If a business wants to stay in business, it cannot just think of today's bottom line, it must make a company commitment to help others immediately. By helping others, you are creating future customers and inspiring employee loyalty. Customers like to be involved with people and businesses that donate their time to help others and make a difference." His inspired, personal relationships with the people he leads have kept them around while keeping his companies on top. He helped develop them into leaders by investing in their future and allowing them to grow and achieve their personal and professional goals.

Camaraderie and Celebration

A fascinating analysis from *Harvard Business Review* details Dr. Emma Seppälä's findings about workplace happiness and productivity: "A positive work climate also leads to a positive workplace culture which, again, boosts commitment, engagement, and performance. Happier employees make for not only a more congenial workplace but for improved customer service. As a consequence, a happy and caring culture at work not only improves employee well-being and productivity but also improved client health outcomes and satisfaction."[50] This happiness she speaks of comes directly from empathy, values, and a willingness of leaders to build positive relationships.

Finally, Chester Elton and Adrian Gostick, authors of *The Carrot Principle* and *All In*, point out the importance of celebrating in a team environment. The benefits of camaraderie and encouragement are currency that go a long way toward engendering a culture of togetherness and optimism. Celebrating the wins—both big and small—helps to recognize your employees and provide them with a feeling of belonging: "Cheering is unifying. It creates an atmosphere of camaraderie and a willingness to accept each other and buoy one another. It acknowledges that each person on the team, by himself, will be unsuccessful unless everyone works together in a balanced, concerted effort."[51]

No matter where you're trying to go as an emotionally intelligent leader, remember to heed the African proverb: "If you want to go fast, go alone. If you want to go far, go together." Think of that when you consider the culture you aim to mold and form for your team and company.

Culture Exercise:
Calling the Shots

The goal here is to stretch your creative thinking. This exercise will improve your preparation and holistic thinking toward inclusiveness.

You just received a promotion! Congratulations! You're the new vice president tasked with leading multiple business units at your organization. The first item of business is to address 100 employees in the upcoming monthly All Hands meeting. Your employees expect you to provide strategic direction, but also want to learn your vision for the organization's culture. Morale is low and numerous director-level employees have recently left. How will you reshape the culture to turn things around? Write your plans in three to five sentences.

Culture Exercise:
Culture in Action

Who has modeled the attributes of emotionally intelligent leadership that you've admired in your career? What type of impact did they have on the organization? Revisit each of your career stops. If you've only been with one organization, think of the leaders you've encountered. You may also use examples of leaders you've observed from a distance. What did they do well (or not well!) in each of the following five areas?

- Self-awareness

- Self-regulation

- Motivation

- Empathy

- Social skill

Culture Exercise: Team Builder

You're mixing things up in this week's team meeting. In an effort to have some fun mixed with team bonding, you're introducing a new team-building exercise. Come up with an activity that will get people talking, thinking, laughing, and lead to additional conversation. Make sure this exercise connects to the vision and values of your organization.

On Diversity

In 2020, emotionally intelligent leaders have an open mind and prominently include diversity and inclusion as part of their organizational vision. Long gone are the days of neglecting the needs of employees who ask for help. Preemptively, it's critical that an emotionally intelligent leader creates and cultivates a culture of acceptance, empowerment, and understanding. Diversity encompasses many categories including gender, age, race, or ethnicity. For the emotionally intelligent leader, showing tolerance and empathy for all employees is a mind-set that permeates the organization.

As described by leaders from the Emotional Intelligence and Diversity Institute, "creating an emotionally intelligent work environment involves creating a balance between having shared organizational values and honoring individual uniqueness."[52] This balance takes time to achieve, like any desired cultural change, and is brought about through programs and forums where employees can openly share their individual uniqueness. A strong culture engenders an environment that values creativity and authenticity, while eschewing limitations that prevent this from taking root.

(continued)

Companies that embrace diversity don't just talk about it; they act and set measurable goals to achieve this. As Forbes points out, "Several organizations such as Google and Facebook publish their annual diversity report, which details what progress they have made with their D&I goals, as well as areas for improvement."[53]

CEO Sheila Lirio Marcelo, founder of Care.com (whose story you'll learn more about in this chapter), has said that diversity "improves productivity, performance and stock price in the long term. Diversity proves that things can be better. Own the differences, and then they are absolutely strengths."[54] Marcelo owned what made her different from her mostly white, male colleagues, and used the strengths of her family, cultural, and business background to turn Care.com into a multi-billion-dollar enterprise. Along the way, she's served as a role model for every woman of color to never accept the status quo, but instead to dream bigger and bolder.

According to scholars at the Emotional Literacy Foundation, "The model of emotional intelligence and diversity (EID) . . . encompasses the ability to feel, understand, articulate, manage, and apply the power of emotions to interactions across lines of difference. Diversity, those aspects of individual traits across which individuals and teams interact, helps people understand the multiple dimensions of individuality across which people see similarities and differences. Dealing with others across these lines of difference often triggers powerful responses that require emotional intelligence to manage."[55]

There is much ground to make up, particularly in industries like tech, manufacturing, and finance, but taking action and bringing issues to the fore makes it easier to create awareness that drives progress. Efforts made by leaders like Sheila Lirio Marcelo have promoted diversity in the workplace and given hope to many leaders of color that the playing field is getting a bit more level.

Reality vs. Vision

Let's get our hands dirty! It's time to dive right into the details. Here, we'll design a roadmap for how *you* can begin to shift the dynamics of making your organization a more emotionally intelligent one.

We're going to focus on four phases of turning your vision into reality. We'll start with the basics, and what better place to begin than creating your vision for the direction you want to lead?

- Establish the basics that determine your desired standard.
  - Vision
  - Purpose
  - Mission
  - Core values

- Focus on your people.
  - Identify what makes you unique and what your strategic goals are
  - Model this behavior and influence your employees to adopt it
  - Establish what you desire for your people—their personal and professional development
  - Create an environment of diversity, inclusiveness, and belonging that shows you care
  - Provide open, candid forums for feedback and partnership with all levels of employees

- Communicate, communicate, communicate!
  - Make sure expectations are clear and understood
  - Tie your strategic goals and desired results back to your core values, vision, purpose, and mission, and make sure you gain alignment organization-wide
  - Create key performance indicators for business units

- Communicate performance management objectives for each individual and ensure that managers and leaders have regular check-ins on personal and professional development with employees

- Develop a constantly self-improving and innovating mind-set and approach.
  - Evaluation and reflection at the core of each step
  - How can we do things better?
  - Celebrate the wins!

Call this your "Blueprint for an Emotionally Intelligent Organization" and think deeply about how you can apply this *today*. We're often held back by that little voice inside our heads that threatens to derail us when we're on the cusp of something special. Don't let fear hold you back, especially if you've already spent several years at your company. I've coached leaders who are now leading staff that were once their peers. Yes, it can be uncomfortable at first, but part of being an emotionally intelligent leader is demonstrating maturity and professionalism. Professionals look to the present and future with equanimity by keeping an open mind and communicating expectations with empathy and thoughtfulness.

Wherever you are, this blueprint will empower you to lead from the front with authority, self-awareness, and dedication to serving the needs of your employees. Turning a vision into reality begins with getting those you lead to adopt the behavioral changes you want to see. Express your vision for the future and gain buy-in by sharing other examples of success, or times you've achieved success in similar situations. Get firm on your basics. Gather input from the organization and make this an inclusive process. Make your decision based on input from these sources, and then use the best information at hand to determine culture and strategic direction.

Reality vs. Vision Exercise: Change Task Force

Identify a list of 5 to 10 "champions" you have met or developed a relationship with throughout the organization. Create a Change Task Force of these individuals who can amplify your message and become multipliers throughout the organization. The most important thing is to find people you trust, that you've formed authentic relationships with, and who truly believe in you and your message.

Set up regular meetings with this task force and ask for their input throughout the effort. Create a communications strategy they can execute throughout the organization to ensure success.

Reality vs. Vision Exercise: One-Page Plan

Put together a one-page plan of your vision for the things that need to be improved in your organization, business unit, or across your team. Explain *how* you plan to address these issues by incorporating an emotionally intelligent approach. Be succinct. Break it down into these areas:

- Strategy

- Process

- Culture

What thoughts come to mind as you reflect upon what you've written?

Reality vs. Vision Exercise: Change Control

This exercise provides clarity around where it is best to spend your time. For your change effort, organize topics into these three categories:

- Things you can control

- Things you can influence

- Things you cannot control

The things you can control will likely seem obvious to you. For example, you can control the frequency of and methods with which you communicate to the organization. However, the power of this exercise is to recognize what you *can* influence and what you *cannot* control.

You can influence the champions and team leads around you by encouraging and supporting them. This is where empathy and social skill come in.

You cannot control whether an individual user takes action, but you can do your best to set them up for success and have regular check-ins.

Understand these three, and you will know where to focus your time, energy, and resources.

Vision to Reality

Cultural change can take several years, so it's important to exercise patience as you take your vision to reality. Norm Sabapathy, EVP of People at Cadillac Fairview, said, "It doesn't happen overnight. It really depends on assessing the true gap between the culture you have and the culture you need to have."[56] The nuance of change is understanding just how much actually needs to be changed, strategically and tactically. Sometimes this cultural change will enhance productivity and, ultimately, reputation.

Few examples of change are more remarkable than the joint auto plant that General Motors (GM) and Toyota shared in Fremont, California, New United Motor Manufacturing, Inc., more well known as NUMMI. It's the story of how Toyota's production system was implemented and embraced by GM, with dazzling results. The venture began in 1984 and lasted until 2010 and epitomized lean manufacturing. American employees in Fremont, California, wholeheartedly embraced the Toyota system that highly values each employee, giving them a sense of job security, self-confidence, and respect. The system motivates, empathizes, and breeds connection. It's a fascinating study in how a proven vision became reality in an environment where it didn't seem possible.

John Shook, chairman and CEO of the Lean Enterprise Institute, said, "The Union and workers didn't just accept Toyota's system, they embraced it with passion. The absenteeism that had regularly reached 20 percent or more? It immediately fell to a steady 2 percent. The quality that had been GM's worst? In just one year, it became GM's best. All with the exact same workers. The only thing that changed was the production and management system—and somehow, the culture."[57]

Another brilliant example of cultural turnaround comes from Anne Mulcahy, a pioneer of leadership during her nearly eight years at the helm of Xerox. She dramatically turned around the fortunes of an organization that was on the precipice of disaster. Xerox went from a household name in printing for nearly 100 years to facing Chapter 11 bankruptcy. Mulcahy had been at Xerox for 25 years and had built great relationships. She had an honest, grassroots vision for the company that she turned into reality by leading from the heart and communicating across the organization.

One unconventional way she helped turn her vision into reality was by crafting a fictitious *Wall Street Journal* article that was a blueprint for the future of what Xerox wanted to achieve. She included things like performance metrics and major goals, soliciting the feedback of many employees who knew what had previously made the organization great.

It was a bold move. It was inspiring. It worked. In an interview, Mulcahy said, "I asked for it. I sat down with 100 of our top executives, was completely honest with them about the state of the company, and then asked them whether they were willing to fight with me. I told them they'd have my blessing if they chose to leave, but that I needed fighters by my side. All but two of them stuck with the company. It was such an uplifting moment."[58]

Xerox returned to being a profitable company in less than 18 months, all while improving its research and development efforts and decreasing its debt. It started making smarter decisions that were informed by Mulcahy's vision, which came from building relationships, communicating, and leading with empathy. "I visited offices, I rode with salespeople, I fostered ongoing conversations between senior managers to problem-solve—I did everything I could think of to create relationships both within and outside of our organization. Because in the end, your relationships will save you. You cannot build loyalty without building relationships. And that's what it took to turn the tide at Xerox: loyalty, and determination, and passion for our company. Everyone had to feel empowered to give their all, and feel accountable to each other for the results. They did, and it worked."[59]

Extraordinary leaders like Anne Mulcahy know that in order to turn a vision into reality, you leave no stone unturned.

Obstacles

One of the first obstacles every leader faces is resistance to change. Ingrained in the culture of almost every organization is an attitude that—in some way, shape, or form—is resistant to change. It may not be acknowledged, and employees may not be aware of it, but that doesn't mean it's not there. Resistance to change can very easily creep in and become the reason a great company fails. As we saw earlier, Eastman Kodak was unwilling to adapt to major changes in technology. Sometimes the change can be quite subtle, such as the process for creating a product, or the implementation of a professional service. Stagnant processes become resistant to change.

The culture of one of the world's largest, most successful companies is so admired there have been books written about it—*The Apple Way* among them. How does a company of more than 130,000 employees have a "way" of doing business? It's embodied in the spirit of its founder, Steve Jobs, who was an innovator who stopped at nothing to ensure that his company was always evolving, inventing, and changing the way we consume technology products. That "way" attracts an entrepreneurial, self-aware spirit in Apple employees that is always willing to overcome mental and emotional stagnation in an effort to put forward the very best products. Apple's innovation is about providing customers with products they didn't quite know they wanted—truly cutting edge.

Overcoming Ourselves and Our Environment

Emotionally intelligent leaders overcome obstacles by recognizing their mission is about something bigger than themselves. Sheila Lirio Marcelo, founder and CEO of Care.com, leads an enormously successful company and has also helped female entrepreneurs and empowered women by launching Womenup.org and Landit.com. Her success is astounding, and yet we may remember her most for the tremendous obstacles she overcame to simply have a seat at the table that has long been dominated by men.

The bias against women in the workforce has existed for a long time, and still does. Marcelo's story is one of incredible meaning and value to women, and particularly women of color. She started Care.com largely because she was having a challenging time finding care for her own child. She learned from other moms that this was the case for them. Using her business acumen and desire to help others, she founded a company that helped create the marketplace she desired. "As women, we fear that our role as caregivers is something that we need to hide from our employers because we feel like we are going to be judged," she said. "We need to change that because, in reality, the role of caregiving actually drives this economy."[60]

By focusing on people's needs and pains, she found her passion, but first she simply had to overcome the obstacle of being a Filipina woman who was often discriminated against. Marcelo has told several stories of how throughout her career men assumed she was the assistant, or there to provide them with coffee.[61] Some men assumed she knew little because she was a woman. Insulting, to say the very least. This is a sad truth many women—particularly women of color—have had to overcome for too long. By putting diversity front and center, and acknowledging that these obstacles must be overcome, leaders like Sheila Lirio Marcelo help women everywhere reclaim their self-worth.

The Will to Change

We've seen that a major obstacle to change can be the process—the "business as usual" way of doing things. Sometimes people are identified as the problem. It's harder for people to change once they've become entrenched in an organization and they get used to one way of doing things. An important reason people can become obstacles is linked to motivation. Psychologist Frederick Herzberg's "two-factor theory" shows that while some workplace factors cause job satisfaction, others cause dissatisfaction. Motivating factors that can cause satisfaction, for example, are things like recognition, reward, an opportunity to truly make a difference, and empowerment for decision-making that leads to tangible, positive results.

Without these motivating factors present, people can lose their shared interest and seek only their own personal interest. This leads to a resistance to change that contributes to an overall culture that doesn't want change. This means that one of the biggest obstacles to change is often misconstrued. It's not accurate to simply say, "It's the people." It's often the process by which information is disseminated, thus making it a leadership problem.

As *New York Times* bestselling author Mark Murphy points out, it's usually executives who are more willing to change, whereas frontline employees are less likely: "The data is pretty clear that frontline employees are going to be less excited by change than top executives. In fact, every role except managers is significantly less excited about change than the top executives. And yet, which role do executives converse with most frequently? Other executives!"[62]

Think about that—it's the method rather than a problem of one specific group. When you don't involve everyone and only concern yourself with people at the top, the result can easily be a major obstacle to change.

I've developed four criteria to focus on as an emotionally intelligent leader to avoid obstacles that stand in the way of successfully leading your organization:

First, stop making excuses. Acknowledge obstacles for what they are. This begins with what we tell ourselves. Acknowledge inherent biases for what they are, address them, and become a champion for changing things that stand in the way of you and your employees' success. Speak positively. Tell yourself you can do it, and then tell others. Commit and figure out how.

Second, take initiative! You may assume your employees won't want to change, but how will you really know until you try? Adopt the Anne Mulcahy playbook and ramp up your "boots on the ground" strategy. Get out in front of things, communicate, empathize, influence, and take those inputs to inform your decision-making.

Third, remember that "the buck stops here." President Harry S. Truman popularized this phrase, and it's one that every emotionally intelligent leader should heed. For our purposes, this is all about the self-management side of emotional intelligence: OWN IT. Don't pass the buck. Be visible. Let people know you're in charge. Couple this with humility and courage and you'll earn everyone's respect.

Finally, celebrate the victories! Share in the successes along the way. Bring people together by making it about the team.

Obstacles Exercise:
Identifying the Challenges

Identify the top challenges you face, either in a new change effort or as you reshape your organization to be more emotionally intelligent. Group these challenges into the following categories:

- Leadership

- Process

- Communication

- Technology

- Resources

The best thing a leader can do is provide clarity for his or her employees. By understanding the challenges, you can assess what needs to be incorporated in your change management plan so you can address and resolve them.

Obstacles Exercise:
Town Hall Discussion

Organize a town hall discussion of diverse professionals representing different races, ethnicities, genders, and religions. Create the structure for a one-hour forum where you ask employees to speak about the obstacles they've faced and the current challenges they find in their roles.

Choose a facilitator, set a time limit of one to two minutes for each speaker, and provide opportunities for follow-up questions. Ask each employee to conclude with solutions to help make their path and career at the company better. The goal is to walk away with actionable strategic recommendations to implement to help support your diverse workforce.

Obstacles Exercise:
Obstacles Checklist

Use this checklist as a reference to identify and address obstacles to executing your strategy:

- ☐ Employees resistant to change
- ☐ Culture unwilling to adapt
- ☐ Scope of change effort is not clear
- ☐ Adoption of new technology that employees don't understand
- ☐ Little to no communication
- ☐ Lack of buy-in from frontline managers
- ☐ Employees don't understand "why" or benefits
- ☐ Poor (or lack of) governance structure
- ☐ Change Task Force or leadership team not in place (or not visible)
- ☐ Overall frustration on length of time and scope
- ☐ Political factions
- ☐ Fear of job loss/layoffs

Takeaways

When it comes to how you choose to lead, one adage is certain: Don't let yourself become the obstacle. Look inward and make sure your leadership is not serving as an impediment. Everything begins with how you communicate with others. While harder at larger organizations, it's still achievable to connect with everyone from the executive level to the frontline employees, both electronically and in person. You simply have to make the time for it!

For leaders, the core components of successful change are motivation and social skill, along with empathy and self-awareness. It's not enough to communicate to your team and only rely upon them. Make sure your message travels far and wide.

Are the biggest obstacles people or process? It's a bit of both, though more often the process is the obstacle. Most employees genuinely seek to support the greater good of the organization.

CHAPTER SIX

Sustaining Change

Here's a very simple success formula that will illuminate your leadership perspective: Commitment + Consistency + Momentum = Impact

Getting started is about initiative and commitment to building a leadership culture. To sustain change, through words and actions you'll need to consistently apply empathy, encouragement, respect, and connection. This develops momentum, bringing stakeholders onboard and creating electric, positive energy that carries your leadership efforts forward. Do this and you will have left an indelible impact on the organization you lead.

We'll focus on consistency by highlighting what you need to do to check in on your efforts, to focus on the process, and to make adjustments, knowing there will be roadblocks along the way. Sustaining change requires continuity and consistency, with a backbone of adaptability. We see this in the remarkable story of Swiss company Victorinox, an organization that adapted, grew, and remains strong 135 years after its founding. Through the eyes of extraordinary leaders who have instilled winning cultures, we'll see what it means to learn, grow, and lead while technology, social norms, and business needs evolve.

Checking In

Emotionally intelligent leaders know that success can be elusive if you choose one path and never deviate as the playing field shifts. This applies to us individually and to the organizations we lead. Adaptability is at the heart of every great change initiative, and equally at the core of our own perpetual reinvention. Leading with emotional intelligence means up-leveling your skills, learning something new, and making shifts that show a mindfulness toward your surroundings.

We must reinvest in ourselves as leaders by using tools like the Game Plan on page 74 and seeking new inputs that improve our leadership toolkit. Adjust and advance is the name of the game. Likewise, leading an organization, department, division, or even a small unit requires adjustments. It's not so much about following a playbook as it is about gaining a deep understanding of four key areas of your business:

- Your people
- Your customers
- Your strategy
- Your culture

Focus on the business side too much and you risk losing the people you lead. Focus too much on reputation and you risk losing customers and profit. There must be a balance and all-encompassing approach to leadership that is well-planned and focused on achieving growth. The surest way to get there is to keep these priorities top of mind. Plan balance into your day and week that is authentic and true to your core values. This self-management component of having a plan and executing it with both IQ and EQ is critical.

Champions

Who are the champions? They are the trusted advisers, high performers, and yes, coaches, that you can come to for honest, positive, self-improving feedback. They encourage and inspire you, but won't be afraid to level with you and tell it like it is. You need champions on board for any successful transformation and change endeavor. They will sustain the momentum of the change effort and continue to gain more change agents, influencers, and champions to support the overall strategic goals. This is why it's not just important to find these people at the beginning of your venture, but to maintain these connections and build these relationships throughout.

Attracting and recruiting champions takes moxie, confidence, empathy, and authenticity. Employees can smell a phony from miles away. The art of relationship-building is continuous, as you need to demonstrate that your call for help is crafted for the collective good. How do you bring these champions on board, the supporters who will stand behind you, communicate, and leverage your ideas? It's best to follow a simple acronym I use in my coaching work and set the "BAR" high: Believe, Achieve, Rapport.

To get employees to follow and continue following, you need to give them a reason to *believe* in what you're doing. If they trust you, you're halfway there. But you must convince them of the purpose and continue to update them. Everyone needs to know what you're striving to *achieve*, so the results must always be front and center. Last, the *rapport* you have with champions and supporters is everything. This is built on empathy, and it's solidified with engagement and follow-through.

Relationships are hard to build when you need them. I've seen this throughout my career. Authentic business relationships are built on curiosity, candor, and a willingness to help. An emotionally intelligent leader makes a point to schedule purpose-driven, productive meetings with as many people in their organization as possible. They meet the sales reps, marketing and communications teams, project managers, product development, finance, HR, and mailroom teams. This shows an understanding and depth that's built on empathy and led by social skill that says, "I want to know you and help you grow here."

Forging relationships helps increase our mental inventory of knowledge. We learn what will work in this environment and what won't. We gather knowledge on organizational politics, leadership, and history. Remember: So much of what defines success as a leader is learning the company history, finding what makes people tick, and showing a genuine desire to help.

Learning to Adapt

Adaptability is the core component of emotional intelligence that comes into play during a change initiative. This ability helps you understand and recognize the three phases outlined in this chapter. It's not enough for you to become comfortable with the change, even though it starts with you as a leader. "Buy-in" relies on your social skills of persuasion and empathy to help employees see three things:

- Their role in the process
- The importance of the change and how it can and will positively or negatively influence them (be honest and present all the facts)
- Their individual duty to help drive the change

During any change effort, help your employees understand that this is an opportunity for them. The most dynamic change efforts incentivize employees to step up and create leadership opportunities for themselves. As an organization moves into the future, it wants future-minded players who are going to capitalize on the need for change.

Keeping a Positive Mind-Set

There's a ubiquitous myth that most change efforts fail, so it's not surprising that many organizations employ steering committees and consultants, and prepare massive communications efforts in advance. It's just as important to sustain these efforts as it is to continue with coaching, communication, and support during the process, particularly as employees start to feel fatigue—or worse yet, burnout.

Organizational psychologist and keynote speaker Nick Tasler has plenty of experience researching major change efforts. The results that he's found are stunning. He writes in *Harvard Business Review*: "As leaders . . . we need to be aware that our team members are not entering change situations with a blank slate. Two decades of hearing about mythical failure rates has planted the seeds of bias against success in our minds. And every time we say 'change is hard' we water those seeds.

By priming people with a simple fact about the high probability of successful change, the researchers completely eliminated the negative bias. In a series of studies, University of Chicago researchers found that we assume that failure is a more likely outcome than success, and, as a result, we wrongly treat successful outcomes as flukes and bad results as irrefutable proof that change is difficult."[63]

Recognize that a major part of checking in is coaching your employees through the change, and consistently providing positive direction. It's not enough just to do this in the beginning—stick to your plan throughout, and as always, know how to adapt when needed.

Checking-In Exercise: Feedback

With your direct supervisor, analyze feedback you've received. For a baseline, use your most recent annual assessment. Divide the feedback into three areas:

- Themes

- Areas to improve

- Three main goals for this year

Focusing on these three areas and having them in writing will help you become intimately aware of your strengths, address the areas you need to improve, and perform your own personal gap analysis to take you from where you are now to where you want to be.

Once you've identified the three biggest goals you want to achieve in the year ahead, write down the success measures that will support you in achieving those goals.

Checking-In Exercise: Performance Evaluation

It's time to evaluate the change initiative taking place. Answer these three questions as honestly and objectively as you can, and then pose them to the frontline managers in the field and/or the Change Task Force you've assembled:

- What's gone well?

- What hasn't?

- What can be improved?

Balance these answers against key performance indicators and request specific examples. Turn the improvements into strategic recommendations that can be used in the overall management of the change effort.

Checking-In Exercise: Modification

You're now 6 to 12 months into your change initiative. Revisit your change management plan—specifically, the objectives and goals that you started with. Which goals no longer make sense? What should be added? Do you need to modify and make adjustments to your plan? Think big picture here. This exercise will provide clarity and honesty about prioritization.

Roadblocks to Change

The roadblocks to change center around two areas: resources and communication.

Resources: Let's define resources as people and funding. On the people side, make sure the biggest impediment to progress isn't you! This is why we always begin with self-awareness. Your vision should allow you to clearly understand the challenges you face so you can prioritize your time around the most important items—the "biggest rocks"—each day. Less important issues should be delegated to others so that your focus always aligns with your values, mission, and goals. Take care of yourself first.

When change has not worked in the past, sometimes employees can develop a cynical or jaded feeling. Make sure that you're starting fresh, developing enthusiasm and positive energy by connecting with as many of your employees as possible. Connection breeds champions, and you need champions (as discussed earlier), not detractors.

Look for employees who show the most initiative. Gather information through surveys, focus groups, voluntary meetings, and by empowering employees to step up and become change leaders. Focus your energy on building relationships seeded with empathy and a genuine desire to help your employees achieve their goals. Highlight employees who show drive, ambition, and initiative—all marks of emotionally intelligent leaders (motivation and positive outlook stand out here).

Communication: As George Bernard Shaw said, "The single biggest problem in communication is the illusion that it has taken place." A change initiative is doomed to fail if you are unable to communicate the before, during, and after stages of what you're doing. Err on the side of over-communicating—becoming repetitive—to make sure you're both inclusive and comprehensive in addressing what you're doing. Not only is this wise during a change initiative, it's a good business practice to implement at all times!

Follow communication and change best practices to ensure success. Be succinct, clear, and demonstrate the results and value you're striving to achieve. You don't want people to tune you out during long, drab, hard to understand speeches. Be direct and honest in all that you do while helping people understand exactly what is taking place. Remember—be repetitive! Time your efforts right, and allow time for them to be achieved.

In one of the biggest, worst examples of a change initiative, AOL Time Warner failed largely because of poor communication and a lack of sensitivity to merging two very different cultures. It didn't take long for both sides to realize that they didn't share the same vision for the future. You might wonder how they didn't know that in advance! Simply put, the two sides came from different worlds and didn't communicate well. As noted in Fortune, "The aggressive and, many said, arrogant AOL people 'horrified' the more staid and corporate Time Warner side. Cooperation and promised synergies failed to materialize as mutual disrespect came to color their relationships."[64]

Make sure that you over-communicate and align people with the nuances of cultural impact, or you risk failure from the beginning.

Process

What is the secret of the most successful leaders in all industries? If we were to boil it down very succinctly, it would be these two things:

1. An incredible attention to detail

2. An ability to adapt to change

Leaders with these qualities always remain mindful of the culture they're building and how to sustain the gains they've made. The culture you create establishes how you treat your people, and how focused you are on every detail of the process that leads to the achievement of your strategic goals.

In the world of sports, we find a leader with an incredible devotion to winning inch-by-inch and mastering each step of the process. To win at a championship level, you need to establish a culture, system, and process that is always being refined and evaluated. Coach Bill Belichick has won six Super Bowls and competed in nine, largely due to a remarkable love and commitment to the process of winning. It started with the culture he built with the New England Patriots, which manifested in attracting, drafting, and developing players who wanted to constantly improve—and win. Belichick has constantly adapted and evolved to manage football strategy, tactics, player relationships, and diffusing turmoil each season. Any time he sees the Patriots organization isn't on track, he immediately steps in to address the issue.

Coach Belichick may not be the first person we think of when it comes to emotionally intelligent leadership, largely due to his aloof appearances with the media, but the more you study the man's success, it's easy to recognize the way his emotions inform his decisions. He's remarkably self-aware and he cares deeply about his players and the integrity of his team. He constantly motivates his players to get better, and lets them know he cares about their success. He's an innovator who is always looking for ways to improve.

Early in his career, Belichick wasn't a great champion. He had only one winning season in his first six as a head coach. He learned from tough losses that he needed to adapt; it wasn't enough to be a very knowledgeable coach. What mattered more was how he formed connections with veterans and new players. He built "champions" in time-tested veteran players he knew he could trust. He leveraged their influence to form a continuous evolution of motivation, teamwork, and a high standard of expectation from player to coach to every member on his staff.

Belichick focused on every detail of the process and every person in the football operation. He obsessed over all the small details, getting every member of the organization to believe in and implement his system. In doing so, he has built a culture where, from the top to the bottom, winning is an obsession.

Grassroots Leadership

Let's mix things up and take a look at political campaigning. The way a politician effectively reaches and influences constituents can provide insights and inform our leadership. While we can all agree to disagree on various issues and candidates, one thing we can unanimously agree upon is a grassroots communications strategy of reaching out and forming meaningful connections with as many stakeholders as possible.

There's power in numbers, yes, and also power in the impact of every touchpoint you have. Political candidates cast the net wide and then hit the ground to meet as many potential voters as possible. As a leader, your influence and reach need to extend far beyond the campaign trail once you assume a new role. It's critical that you check in and understand whether you should stay the course on your change effort or change direction. Set reminders and always be cognizant of owning the relationships that you have on your team and throughout the organization.

Acclaimed CEO Fred Hassan, who formerly led three pharmaceutical companies, advised "singling out frontline managers as a critically important group in the management ranks, spending significant personal time in direct interactions with them, and using those interactions to mobilize the entire organization. I call this approach leading through the front."[65]

(continued)

Let's translate "leading through the front" by examining its virtues. What does it achieve?

- It gets everyone involved in the process
- It shows genuine empathy and interest in people's concerns, problems, and key issues
- It communicates respect

By taking the time to meet people across all departments, functions, and roles, you're demonstrating an egalitarian approach toward getting to know people. You're showing that you care and are leading with respect. Kristie Rogers, assistant professor of management at Marquette University, speaks about this in an interview with *Harvard Business Review*: "Owed respect is simply the way that people are treated with a level of civility, with a basic regard that is professional, that is decent . . . Earned respect is something that's recognized as valued achievements, valued attributes of a particular person and gives them a chance to be unique, to stand out in a positive way. Those two types of respect meet different universal needs that we have."[66]

Think about the times you've felt respected, admired, and recognized for good work you did. Doesn't it feel good? When it's missing, we yearn, consciously and subconsciously, to receive it. It motivates, inspires, and gives us perspective on how we're doing. It feels good and makes us want to perform better. Its absence can lead to stagnation and a feeling that we're out of the loop—or at worst, it's perceived as a form of disrespect.

Emotionally intelligent leaders aren't just salespeople, ribbon cutters, or hand shakers. They lead with authenticity by keeping employees informed on the details, understanding their needs, and showing candor and curiosity to learn more about those they lead. They exude confidence and don't waver in providing direction when things don't succeed at first.

These aren't just suggestions or ideas for sustaining successful change initiatives. You might even call them requirements.

Process Exercise:
Process Improvement Guide

Review your processes and highlight areas for improvement:

- Scope: Ensure the focus is on the essential areas for improvement

- Cost: Determine whether money is being allocated and spent efficiently

- Time: Is the schedule on track for completion of the project? What holdups and delays can be mitigated or eliminated to ensure success?

- Quality: Review results and tasks against key performance indicators to measure quality standards

- Communication: Is the message getting across? What tools can you better leverage and use to your advantage?

- People management: Are you and your leadership team shepherding employees through this process successfully?

Process Exercise:
Halftime Scoreboard

The statements below are probably true to some degree, but how can you do better? Think honestly about how well you are doing these things, and identify ways to improve:

- I've done everything I can to meet with all layers of the organization and communicate needs and expectations.

- I've created an environment where the people I lead know their voice and opinion are valued.

- I've put aside my own ego and desires for the greater good of the organization.

- I'm a force of encouragement for the people I lead.

- I take time for perspective-taking and incorporate feedback from others.

- I'm always looking for new, innovative ways to improve our current processes.

Process Exercise: Leadership Retreat

You've been tasked with planning a one-day, off-site leadership retreat for 30 employees (manager-level and above) who are involved in the change initiative you're leading. The goal is to take everyone's minds off the day-to-day and focus on motivating, team-building activities for growth.

Plan three workshops that tie back to the values, purpose, and mission of your organization. Come up with the titles, then list objectives for each one. Focus on activities that will build camaraderie and get team members inspired to achieve their individual and organizational goals.

Adjusting

Emotionally intelligent leaders meet their organizations exactly where they are at any given point. Carl Elsener Jr. found himself needing to do this in crisis mode following the terrorist attacks on New York City on September 11, 2001. His company, Victorinox, found its business challenged like never before. Nearly overnight, sharp objects (namely knives) were prohibited on planes. Even worse, a large percentage of their sales occurred at airport duty-free stores. While not a problem for most companies, it was devastating for this Swiss company. Victorinox is the maker of the world-famous Swiss Army Knife. They seemed doomed. How could they possibly reverse their fortunes?

Founded in 1884, Victorinox had been around for well over 100 years by 2001. A company doesn't stay in business that long without evolving, adapting, and making adjustments along the way. They also sold watches and had begun selling luggage only two years earlier. They diversified their business portfolio and didn't allow an unforeseen event to sink the company.

During that remarkably turbulent time, Victorinox did not fire a single employee. They believed in their core values of being a tight-knit company that supported their people. As CEO Carl Elsener Jr. said, "We lost over 40% of our business . . . Jobs have always been a main focus for us. We really do see ourselves as a big family, in good times and bad."[67]

As the global landscape changed, Victorinox ramped up production of luggage, travel gear, watches, and developed a clothing/leisure line that has since been discontinued. They had the self-awareness to know that their chief product alone wouldn't suffice. An empathetic leader—with seeds of love and care sown in their leader's chair for generations—put his people first. He remained upbeat, positive, and adapted to focus on how to make money in an ever-changing economy. This inspiring vision of adaptation further endeared the brand to millions around the globe.

It's easy to think of Victorinox as a paragon of steadiness during more than a century of dramatic changes in consumer preferences, technology, and international commerce, along with major wars. While they continue to produce the knife that made them famous, it's their ability to adjust to the vicissitudes of world events and the market that showcases the emotional intelligence of their leadership. They know themselves well, and they learned a lesson long ago that has set them up for success now for 135 years: By putting your people first, you can endure in good times and bad.

Getting Back on Track

We know that every change effort needs a little tender love and care, and even then, challenges can remain. Setbacks, delays, and deviations from a change management plan can be costly. As leaders, this is where applying EQ principles can help. Here are some steps to follow when you need a boost to get things back on track:

- Revisit the basics (vision, purpose, mission, and strategic plan goals).

- "Check the pulse": Actively engage with frontline managers and ask them for a pulse check to better understand how employees are feeling. In the midst of an organizational change, ask yourself how you can help employees feel valued, help them understand the change, and actively feel like they're not just executing the strategy, but making a huge difference.

- Storytelling: Share examples of companies that have succeeded. It's easy to lose sight of what's possible, and it helps to balance out your change initiative with positive, game-changing stories of companies that have successfully innovated. Coca-Cola has always kept their mission of innovation front and center. How else can we explain how a soft drink company entered the stratosphere of billions of dollars in sales year after year, and has averaged nearly $40 billion in sales over the past five years?[68] They maintain a highly diverse product line and they're great at listening to their customers.

- Communicate early and often. One thing I tell my executive coaching clients is to be repetitive in their messaging. Think about great advertising campaigns, and the marketing that we all know. We can recite or sing certain companies' slogans or jingles because they're always repeating them. Repeatedly provide strategic direction and clarity, so much so that your employees will never forget it. Better to be known as someone with clear, consistent messaging than a leader who left people out of the loop.

- Define the results and solutions for every key mile marker in the change management process. Use reverse-engineering to understand—first and foremost—the results you are aiming to achieve. Then coordinate with managers on ways to approach this in an all-encompassing manner so that agreed-upon milestones are achieved.

By doing these things, you're aligning your communication efforts with your organizational values and the strategic goals of your change initiative.

What Worked Yesterday
May Not Work Today

As leaders, using emotional intelligence to our advantage entails understanding the art of how to relate to others, when to lead from a certain style, and the results that come from it. Situational leadership, as referenced earlier, enables leaders to get synched up with employees. A strategy that worked three years ago may not work today. This is where it's imperative that leaders have conversations and understand the needs of their teams. When you identify a strategy that needs to be tweaked, recognize that this can have an impact on culture. By engaging regularly with employees, understanding customer needs through tools like Net Promoter Score,[69] and keeping up on market trends, you can successfully gauge how to make decisions and identify opportunities to adjust.

Emotionally intelligent leaders influence and convince people to do new things in a different way by appealing to their emotions, needs, and wants. Some people simply won't follow, no matter what. Others are less pliable and adaptable to the direction that will help move the company forward. Giving in and refusing to try means the battle is lost. The greatest asset is persistence—the will to keep going and continue building relationships, identifying new opportunities for others, and outworking everyone to achieve the desired results.

You have 100 percent operating control over how persistent you are. Cast your worries and fears to the side and keep going when you believe in the vision you've set forth for your organization. Don't worry about being too persistent in your efforts to drive change; you may even ask yourself if you are being persistent enough!

The Queen of Authenticity and Adaptability

Indra Nooyi's journey is one of authenticity, vision, adaptability, and brilliance. She inherited a company that had fallen out of touch with its consumers. She understood that to make the changes she desired for PepsiCo, she needed to significantly alter the company's strategy. She needed her employees on board with these changes, so she promoted an open culture that was powered by empathy. The adjustments she made were due to the connection she built with her employees. Indra Nooyi is nothing short of one of the most successful and beloved CEOs in history. As she said, "Bring people along with you. No matter how smart your strategy, success or failure usually comes down to one thing: the team. In everything you do, find teammates who can help execute your vision and empower them to succeed."[70]

During her tenure, sales grew by 80 percent and the stock price surged, all while Pepsi diversified its portfolio. Remarkably, while turning PepsiCo around she also became beloved among her employees. She believed in them and understood the importance of "hooking them emotionally to the job, through the company's business model and what it stands for. You need to look at the employee and say, 'I value you as a person. I know that you have a life beyond PepsiCo, and I'm going to respect you for your entire life, not just treat you as employee number 4,567.'"[71] She wrote handwritten thank-you notes to her employees, took the time to show her authenticity and values, and made adjustments to culture and strategy that dramatically changed the fortunes of PepsiCo.

CNBC's Jim Cramer said, "She saw the future coming—a future of sustainability and healthy eating—when few others did . . . Her 'Performance with a Purpose' program and her notion of 'doing well by doing good' are her real hallmark. She pioneered the notion of healthier options while reducing greenhouse gas emissions and being at the forefront of diversity."[72]

As Daniel Goleman said, "[Self-regulation] is a competitive asset. We all know the landscape of business changes rapidly. Technology is constantly changing; companies divide and merge every day. At all levels, leaders who know how to self-regulate will thrive on these changes."[73]

Adjusting Exercise: Product and Service Offering Diagnosis

Taking inspiration from the real-life story of Victorinox and how they adapted after 9/11, take a look at your products and/or service offerings for your business.

List each product or service offering and determine which are solid or "recession-proof" and which could be vulnerable to changes in the market or technology. For each item, list the factors that could cause disruption, why it could be vulnerable, and then draft a forward-thinking plan for what you'd do to combat loss of market share or impact to profit. Be honest. This will get you thinking critically about any flaws or shortcomings of what you offer in an effort to stay on top of what you deliver for your customers.

Adjusting Exercise: Drastic Change

You're right near the end of a successful change initiative when your company's stock price starts to plummet. Products have been recalled. Two of your senior-level staff have resigned. Now what? Ask yourself these questions to help guide your next steps:

- What are three activities you can commit to this week (that are measurable) and outcomes you'd like to achieve to help matters?

- What would be the impact on you and the organization if you do nothing?

- What are your biggest communication needs right now?

- What are your biggest people needs right now?

Adjusting Exercise:
Field Work

Your organization is going through another change and your employees are thinking, "Here we go again, another change!" Even you are wondering, "What now?"

Get out in the field. Think about the people in your network—friends, former colleagues, and people you respect. Use LinkedIn and other social media tools to your advantage. Send some emails, make some phone calls, and speak to leaders you respect who have been through significant change efforts. What helped them? What worked? What didn't work? What regrets (if any) do they have?

Personal testimony is powerful. Being able to listen, ask questions, and take notes will help you immensely as you focus on your own change effort.

Takeaways

Every great change initiative is sustained by the champions who communicate and act upon the vision of their leader. First and foremost, find champions in your organization that you can rely on and turn to throughout the process. Finding these champions early on during your tenure—and continuing to cultivate these relationships—will open the doors to powerful relationships. People make change efforts possible, and it's always best to let your people know they are highly valued.

Keep a positive mind-set and stay nimble and agile. Coach Bill Belichick and Carl Elsener Jr. led their respective organizations through good times and bad by modifying strategies and putting their people first. By appealing to the emotional needs and wants of the people you lead, you will persevere through any change effort and come out better for it.

Emotional Intelligence Assessments

In this section are the assessments that you found in chapter 2. Assessing each pillar of emotional intelligence, these questions will help you understand where you are currently and allow you to see where you want to be. Like any assessment—whether these or other well-known assessments like DISC, CliftonStrengths, or MBTI—they are only meant to be a snapshot in time. Take them for what they are, whether you perceive them to be good or bad. The data that comes from these will inform you as you continue to cultivate your leadership abilities. Consider sharing your findings with fellow leaders and those you trust. The benefit of shared learning is enormous.

Assessment:
Self-Awareness

To begin, you need to understand the past and present to set your goals. These questions get to the core of who you are currently as a leader:

- What do I do best?

- What am I most passionate about?

- What thoughts come to mind when I think of the way others perceive me?

- What are the three most important things to me in my current role?

- What is my most significant achievement?

- Do I live with regret in my career? If so, why?

- Where do I see myself career-wise when I dream of the best-case scenario?

Take time to reflect; how do your answers mesh with the way you see yourself and the goals you have?

Assessment: Self-Management

Here are the most common emotions:

Positive: joy, gratitude, serenity, interest, hope, pride, amusement, inspiration, awe, and love

Negative: anger, annoyance, frustration, disappointment, fear, despair, guilt, discouragement, anxiety, and envy

For one week, dedicate five minutes per day to writing a list of the emotions you felt, both positive and negative. At the end of the week, reflect on your list. How did you manage yourself in the moment you experienced these emotions? Did they affect your decision-making? Your relationships?

Assessment: Motivation

Honestly answer the following five statements on a scale of 1 (not at all) to 5 (completely):

- I am energized by helping employees to develop personally and professionally.

- I take an interest in coaching others, enabling them to solve problems and achieve solutions through their own self-discovery.

- I keep a positive outlook regardless of present challenges or difficult circumstances.

- I am driven and summon the energy every day to compete to be the best I can for myself and those I lead.

- I take delight in the accomplishments we reach together as a team.

Spend some time analyzing each of these answers and identify specific examples of when you've felt this way. What do you like? What would you improve?

Assessment:
Empathy

Identify 5 to 10 people in your organization whom you know, respect, and can count on to give you objective feedback. Ask them to answer the following five questions on a scale of 1 to 10, with 1 being the lowest or least, and 10 being the highest or most.

- How well do I listen?

- Do I take the time to understand others' positions?

- Do you feel I have invested in others' personal and professional development?

- Do I listen without trying to fix the problem?

- Am I sensitive, compassionate, and caring toward the people I lead?

Assessment:
Social Skill

The statements below are probably true to some degree, but how can you do better? Think honestly about how well you are doing these things, and identify ways to improve:

- I am skilled at persuading colleagues on an idea I believe will help our organization.

- I make influencing the people I lead a focal point for gaining support in the organization.

- I devote time each day to cultivating existing relationships in my inner circle.

- I see myself as a servant leader.

- My colleagues say that I take the time to get to know and understand their needs.

What do you like about the current state of your social skills? What would you improve?

Journal

_____

_____

_____

_____

_____

_____

_____

_____

_____

_____

_____

_____

_____

_____

_____

_____

_____

_____

_____

_____

_____

_____

_____

Resources

http://chrisdconnors.com

My website has an abundance of resources on emotional intelligence and how to make it actionable to build your foundation and game plan.

- Take the 10-question emotional intelligence assessment under "Helpful Tools."
- Fill out your game plan (also included here, in the assessments on page 74).
- Find blogs and links to my best EQ articles, also featured here: https://medium.com/@chrisdconnors
- Executive coaching and seminars: I provide coaching on emotional intelligence for leaders, businesses, and teams. I also offer half-day, full-day, and multi-day emotional intelligence workshops where I partner with executives and organizations to help them reach their goals and build a thriving, emotionally intelligent culture. You're welcome to contact me any time via my website. Please let me know how I can help support you.

Emotional Intelligence by Daniel Goleman

First published in 1995, this book was the first to popularize the concept. This book is a great supplement to what is here in the text. Much of my foundation in the academic and research side of emotional intelligence started with Goleman's findings reported in this book.

How to Win Friends and Influence People by Dale Carnegie

One of the bestselling self-help books of all time, Carnegie's masterpiece is a treasure trove of emotional intelligence. All five pillars of EQ are well-covered here.

CASEL

For academic research on emotional intelligence (or "social and emotional learning"), I recommend visiting https://casel .org/. They're helping to shape the discussion and learning process for students in K-12.

Psychology Today

Want a more in-depth look at your emotional intelligence? I encourage you to take this test: https://www.psychologytoday .com/us/tests/personality/emotional-intelligence-test. It will take you around 45 minutes to complete, but it's well worth the investment of your time and energy. This is an excellent primer for determining self-awareness, empathy, relationship-building skills, passion, and self-management.

Notes

1 Daniel Goleman, **"Emotional Intelligence is a Better Predictor of Success than IQ,"** *Quartz*, May 22, 2013.

2 Peter Economy, **"Sara Blakely's Most Inspiring Quotes for Success,"** *Inc.*, March 20, 2015.

3 Gabrielle Karol, **"How Sara Blakely Built a Billion-Dollar Business from Scratch,"** *Entrepreneur*, October 22, 2014.

4 Simon Sinek, **"How SPANX Fosters Innovation,"** *SimonSays*, Facebook video, April 25, 2018.

5 *The View*, **"Tyler Perry Talks Spiritual Journey, Lessons From Mom, New Projects,"** ABC, aired November 16, 2017.

6 *CBS This Morning*, **"Tyler Perry's 'High is Waiting',"** CBS, aired November 16, 2017.

7 Scott Horner, **"This Celtics team has Butler written all over it,"** *IndyStar*, May 3, 2018.

8 **"Brad Stevens: 2 Keys to Leadership,"** video, PCA Development Zone, Positive Coaching Alliance.

9 **"Talking Teamwork with Celtics Coach Brad Stevens and Angela Duckworth,"** *Heleo*, May 16, 2016.

10 Adam Himmelsbach, **"Brad Stevens Tackles the Puzzle that is the Celtics Rotation,"** *Boston Globe*, October 27, 2015.

11 Sarah Berger, **"ClassPass Founder: This is the Biggest Difference between Successful and Unsuccessful People,"** *CNBC Make It*, July 18, 2018.

12 David Gelles, **"How Payal Kadakia Danced her Way to a $600 Million Start-Up,"** *The New York Times*, August 16, 2019.

13 **"ClassPass' Payal Kadakia's Risk that Changed Her Life,"** *Forbes*, May 5, 2019.

14 **"What is Emotional Intelligence?"** Institute for Health and Human Potential. Accessed February 27, 2020. https://www.ihhp.com /meaning-of-emotional-intelligence.

15 Daniel Goleman, **"How Self-Awareness Impacts Your Work,"** danielgoleman.info, October 4, 2015.

16 Gallup. **"CliftonStrengths."** Accessed February 27, 2020. https://gallup.com/cliftonstrengths/en/252137/home.aspx.

17 Ashley Lee, **"12 Business Leaders on How They Handle Stress,"** *Fortune*, August 30, 2016.

18 Travis Bradberry, **"Why You Need Emotional Intelligence to Succeed,"** *Forbes*, January 7, 2015.

19 **"Intelligence Quotient (IQ),"** Glossary of Important Assessment and Measurement Terms, National Council on Measurement in Education, NCME.org.

20 Paul S. Bellet, MD, and Michael J. Maloney, MD, **"The Importance of Empathy as an Interviewing Skill in Medicine,"** *JAMA Network*, October 2, 1991.

21 Ibid.

22 **"What is Servant Leadership?"** https://www.greenleaf.org/what -is-servant-leadership/.

23 Amelia Harnish and Jessie English, **"Dee Poku-Spalding Turned her Passion Into a Paycheck—& She Wants to Help You Do the Same,"** *Refinery 29*, August 26, 2019.

24 Issie Lapowsky, **"How Pierre Omidyar Turned An Idealistic Notion into Billions of Dollars,"** *Inc.*, December 2013/January 2014.

25 Ibid.

26 Nufer Yasin Ates, Murat Tarakci, Jeanine P. Pork, Daan van Knippenberg, and Patrick Groenen, **"Why Visionary Leadership Fails,"** *Harvard Business Review*, February 28, 2019.

27 Ibid.

28 Don Yaeger, **"Villanova's Jay Wright: How to Sustain Excellence,"** *Forbes*, April 20, 2017.

29 Elizabeth Hopper, **"Can Helping Others Help you Find Meaning in Life?,"** *Greater Good Magazine*, February 16, 2016.

30 Marco della Cava, **"Microsoft's Satya Nadella is Counting on Culture Shock to Drive Growth,"** *USA Today*, February 20, 2017.

31 Ibid.

32 Microsoft. **"About."** Accessed February 27, 2020. Microsoft.com.

33 Vishnu Varma, **"'In the Long Run, EQ Trumps IQ' Microsoft CEO Satya Nadella Tells Students,"** *NDTV*, September 30, 2014.

34 Emma Woollacott, **"Lessons from History's Worst CEOs,"** *CEO Magazine*, July 18, 2018.

35 Associated Press. **"Kay R. Whitmore, 72; Led Eastman Kodak in 90s,"** *The New York Times*, July 29, 2004.

36 **"#55, Katrina Lake,"** *Forbes*, June 3, 2019.

37 Stitch Fix. **"About us."** Accessed February 27, 2020. Stitchfix.com.

38 Nina Zipkin, **"Stitch Fix Founder Explains Why the Worst Piece of Advice She Ever Got Was to Raise a Lot of Money,"** *Entrepreneur*, July 20, 2017.

39 Guy Itzchakov and Avraham N. Kluger, **"The Power of Listening in Helping People Change,"** *Harvard Business Review*, May 17, 2018.

40 Mallory Russell, **"14 Virgin Companies That Even Richard Branson Could Not Stop Going Bust,"** *BusinessInsider*, May 31, 2016.

41 Colin Powell. *It Worked for Me: In Life and Leadership*, New York: Harper Perennial, 2014, 24.

42 Ibid, 25.

43 **"Pyramid of Success,"** CoachWooden.com. Accessed February 27, 2020.

44 **"Situational Leadership,"** Situational.com. Accessed February 27, 2020.

45 Andrew Chamberlain, **"What Matters More to Your Workforce than Money,"** *Harvard Business Review*, January 17, 2017.

46 Michael D. Watkins. *The First 90 Days: Proven Strategies for Getting Up to Speed Faster and Smarter, Updated and Expanded*, Boston: Harvard Business Review Press, 2013.

47 Simon Sinek. *Leaders Eat Last*, Grand Haven, MI: Brilliance Audio, 2017.

48 Christine Porath, **"The Leadership Behavior That's Most Important to Employees,"** *Harvard Business Review*, May 11, 2015.

49 **"Microsoft's Next Act,"** *McKinsey Quarterly*, podcast, April 2018.

50 Emma Seppälä and Kim Cameron, **"Proof That Positive Work Cultures are More Productive,"** *Harvard Business Review*, December 1, 2015.

51 Joyce E. A. Russell, **"Career Coach: Celebrating Small Wins with the Entire Team,"** *The Washington Post*, November 30, 2014.

52 Lee Gardenswartz, Jorge Cherbosque, and Anita Rowe, **"Emotional Intelligence and Diversity: A Model for Differences in the Workplace,"** *Journal of Psychological Issues in Organizational Culture 1*, no. 1 (2010).

53 Janice Gassam, **"The 10 Most Diverse Companies of 2018,"** *Forbes*, October 11, 2018.

54 **"Care.com's Sheila Lirio Marcelo: Overcoming the 'Imposter Syndrome',"** *Knowledge@Wharton*, October 24, 2014.

55 Lee Gardenswartz, Jorge Cherbosque, and Anita Rowe, **"Emotional Intelligence and Diversity: A Model for Differences in the Workplace,"** *Journal of Psychological Issues in Organizational Culture 1*, no. 1 (2010).

56 Christina Folz, **"10 Tips for Changing Your Company's Culture—and Making it Stick,"** *Society for Human Resource Management (SHRM)*, June 27, 2016.

57 John Shook, **"How to Change a Culture: Lessons from NUMMI,"** *MIT Sloan Management Review*, Winter 2010.

58 Bill George, **"Anne Mulcahy: Just Keep Fighting,"** Accessed February 27, 2020. https://discoveryourtruenorth.org/anne-mulcahy-just-keep-fighting/.

59 Ibid.

60 Lisa Wirthman, **"Struggling to Care for Both Parents and Kids? How One Startup Could Help,"** *Forbes*, July 9, 2015.

61 "Care.com's Sheila Lirio Marcelo: Overcoming the 'Imposter Syndrome,'" *Knowledge@Wharton*, October 24, 2014.

62 Mark Murphy, "**New Data Shows That Leaders Overestimate How Much Their Employees Want to Change,**" *Forbes*, February 19, 2016.

63 Nick Tasler, "**Stop Using the Excuse 'Organizational Change is Hard,'**" *Harvard Business Review*, July 19, 2017.

64 Rita Gunther McGrath, "**15 Years Later, Lessons from the Failed AOL-Time Warner Merger,**" *Fortune*, January 10, 2015.

65 Fred Hassan, "**The Frontline Advantage,**" *Harvard Business Review*, May 2011.

66 Kristie Rogers, "**The 2 Types of Respect Leaders Must Show,**" *Harvard Business Review*, July 17, 2013.

67 Wolfgang Koydl, "**How the Swiss Army Knife Survived 9/11,**" *WorldCrunch*, July 20, 2013.

68 "**Coca-Cola Co. NYS: KO,**" Accessed January 16, 2020. Marketwatch.com.

69 Net Promoter Score. https://www.netpromoter.com/know/.

70 Indra Nooyi, "**Parting Words as I Step Down as CEO,**" LinkedIn, October 2, 2018.

71 Raelene Morey, "**How 5 Emotionally Intelligent CEOs Handle Their Power,**" *Pagely*, July 16, 2018.

72 Carmin Chappell, "**Cramer: Outgoing PepsiCo CEO 'Saw the Future Coming' When Few Did,**" CNBC, aired August 6, 2018.

73 Daniel Goleman, "**Self-Regulation: A Star Leader's Secret Weapon,**" danielgoleman.info, July 26, 2015.

Index

Acknowledgments

Thank you to the team at Callisto Media for the vision and guidance to make this book possible. You helped bring my knowledge and passion for emotional intelligence to life. Thank you to my editors Joe Cho, Vanessa Ta, and Lori Handelman for making this a book I'm very proud of.

To my wife, Tosha—I love you and thank you for always leading with empathy for our family. And, oh yeah, showing a lot of patience, too! I marvel at how you've transformed the organization you lead in such a short amount of time. One day soon, I'll be profiling your story as a showcase of emotionally intelligent leadership.

To my two rambunctious, fun-loving boys, Roman and Dominic—you two inspire me every day to give my best and do so with joy in my heart. The greatest leadership gift I've been given is the honor of being your daddy. I'm incredibly excited to meet your younger brother later this year!

Thank you to my mom and dad—I love you and I'm grateful for you each day. You've both taught me so much about emotional intelligence, leadership, believing in myself, and following my passion. You've shown me how to be a great parent. You're the best parents I ever could have asked for. Thank you for your guidance. Thank you for always being there to listen to me. Literally, always. You are my heroes.

Thank you to my brother Kevin, for helping open so many doors for me and for your lifelong friendship. You're a truly great father, husband, son, and brother first—and the best sports broadcaster on television. Thank you to my brother Bill, for your generosity, lifelong friendship, and guidance. You've accomplished many great things—and the best is yet to come. Never give up on your dreams!

Thank you to Ryan Bamford for showing me what it means to run a very successful organization and model emotionally intelligent leadership. Thank you to John Goldman for your guidance, mentorship, and encouragement. Thank you to Sam Shriver of Situational Leadership for your mentorship, kindness, and for believing in me. Thank you to Chris Tate for your guidance and for pushing me to pursue something I love. Thank you to MJ Hall for opening up doors for me and for your incredible kindness. Thank you to Mariam Hutchinson—you're a special friend and someone whose high EQ and grace I deeply admire. Thank you for always believing in me.

I've been remarkably blessed to have had some great mentors in my corner throughout my life. I'm eternally grateful to all of you who have believed in me and shown me the way. I'm also very grateful for friends and partners who have played a role in lifting me up. Special thanks to Kathy Hill, Brian Reilly, Nils Bosch, Brian Punger, LaRhonda Julien, Sarah Cumming, Jackie Allawos, Ron Carman, JT DeNicola, Rob Stewart, and Jasmine Bell.

All of you have inspired me on my own journey of emotional intelligence. I can say unequivocally, the best is yet to come.

About the Author

 **Christopher D. Connors** is a keynote speaker, leadership consultant, executive coach, and emotional intelligence thought leader. Christopher speaks on emotional intelligence and positive leadership for leading organizations. His company, The Value of You Training and Consulting, works with Fortune 500 companies, executives, and schools, providing them with training on emotional intelligence, employee engagement, team building, and culture. His mission is to help leaders grow in emotional intelligence and reach their full potential for themselves and in serving those they lead. His focus on helping people build a rock-solid foundation for living their best life is at the core of all he does. He's the author of *The Value of You: The Guide to Living Boldly and Joyfully through the Power of Core Values.* His writing has appeared on CNBC, World Economic Forum, Quartz, Thrive Global, and Medium. He lives in Charleston, South Carolina, with his beautiful wife and two baseball-loving, rambunctious boys.